W9-BLM-726

MARILYN MOON
and JANEMARIE MULVEY

Entitlements and the Elderly

ENTITLEMENTS AND THE ELDERLY

Protecting Promises, Recognizing Reality

THE URBAN INSTITUTE PRESS
Washington, D.C.

THE URBAN INSTITUTE PRESS
2100 M Street, N.W.
Washington, D.C. 20037

Library of Congress Cataloging in Publication Data

Entitlements and the Elderly: Protecting Promises,
Recognizing Reality / Marilyn Moon and Janemarie Mulvey.

Includes bibliographical references and index.

    1. Old age assistance—United States.   2. Aged—government policy—United States.   3. Aged—medical care—government policy—United States.   I. Mulvey, Janemarie.   II. Title.

HV1461.M66   1995   95-38696
362.6'3'0973—dc20   CIP

ISBN 0-87766-636-9 (cloth, alk. paper)

Printed in the United States of America.

Distributed in North America by:
National Book Network
4720 Boston Way
Lanham, MD 20706

THE URBAN INSTITUTE is a nonprofit policy research and educational organization established in Washington, D.C., in 1968. Its staff investigates the social and economic problems confronting the nation and public and private means to alleviate them. The Institute disseminates significant findings of its research through the publications program of its Press. The goals of the Institute are to sharpen thinking about societal problems and efforts to solve them, improve government decisions and performance, and increase citizen awareness of important policy choices.

Through work that ranges from broad conceptual studies to administrative and technical assistance, Institute researchers contribute to the stock of knowledge available to guide decision making in the public interest.

CONTENTS

Tables

Figures

FOREWORD

As the United States approaches the 21st century, its population is aging and the entitlement programs for the elderly are becoming larger and larger as a proportion of the federal budget. At the same time, there is growing pressure to cut the deficit and balance the federal budget. The congressional budget resolution of June 1995, for example, seeks to balance the federal budget by the year 2002. These two trends appear to be on a collision course.

The purpose of *Entitlements and the Elderly: Protecting Promises, Recognizing Realities* is to take a hard look at how the major entitlements for the elderly can be improved, recognizing the constraints posed by the current budget climate and an aging population. The three major programs the authors consider are Social Security, Medicare, and Medicaid. Medicaid, though not typically referred to in this way, is in fact a major health care entitlement for the low-income elderly. Spending on the elderly under these three programs will constitute about 30 percent of all federal spending in 1995.

Proposals currently pending in Congress would cut $270 billion out of projected spending for Medicare and $182 out of Medicaid over the next seven years. Much of this would perforce involve the elderly if the cuts take place as proposed.

The authors do not take these, or any other specific targets, as their starting point. Rather they contribute to the debate by discussing what changes would make sense on their substantive merits, and then consider what these would reap in the way of savings.

They develop several themes as they go through this exercise. First, it is not necessary or possible to solve all problems over the next few years. What is important is to begin the process in an orderly manner by understanding what future pressures will be. Second, Social Security and Medicare can become more progressive without destroying the principle of social insurance. Third, it is important not to automatically assume everything must be cut. Better targeting can lead to higher spending in some places and large cuts in others. Fourth, and perhaps most important, they make a convincing case that Social Security, Medicare, and Medicaid should be viewed as a whole. They argue, in particular, that thinking about ways to increase progressivity makes no sense until the cumulative effects of the three programs are viewed as a whole.

This book continues the Institute's long-standing commitment to studying ways to improve public policy. It is my hope that the thinking represented here makes a contribution to the current debate both on entitlements for the elderly and on health care financing reform.

William Gorham
President

In this book, we analyze the impact on older Americans of various options that seek to better target the three major entitlements affecting the elderly: Social Security, Medicare and Medicaid. Our interest is in improving the effectiveness of these intrinsically valuable programs while recognizing that there are important pressures to scale back their overall size. We look for ways to improve these programs, recognizing that there are constraints imposed by both the current federal budget climate and the future financing challenges of an aging population. Moreover, Social Security, Medicare and Medicaid are importantly interrelated. As a consequence, we examine all three, recognizing that this prevents us from considering all possible options for changing any one program. In a sense, by taking on three major policy areas, we do not explore any one in depth, but we still believe it important to take this broader view.

Our basic premise is to examine what policy options make most sense rather than to seek ways to meet some dollar target for savings. While the timing of this book might instead suggest a concentration on how to achieve such a target reduction in spending on entitlements as part of a balanced federal budget strategy—an issue much in the news as this preface is being written—we do not approach the issues in this way. A seven year goal of $270 billion in reduced spending on Medicare and $182 billion in savings from Medicaid—as specified in the Budget Resolution passed by the Congress in the spring of 1995—will require changes beyond what we believe are reasonable goals for the future. And if our hypothesis on that is correct, these targets will be modified in future years to reflect more realistic levels of change. It is in that context that we believe this volume can be of most help.

But we have not ignored the present political discourse. Consequently, we do address many of the options and issues now being discussed and thus some of our analysis should be helpful in finding ways to cut back the programs. And, some options and approaches for improving entitlements for the elderly that seemed feasible just 18 months ago are now likely to be ignored for some time to come and hence are not always included here.

Work on this project began in 1991, when Judith Feder of Georgetown University and I received a grant from the Retirement Research Foundation to look at ways of improving the targeting of Social Security and Medicare, and then using any savings to help finance improvements in the public funding of long term care. Since the end of the Bush Administration, the policy landscape has changed dramatically—and frequently. Early on, Judy Feder contributed substantially to this work, but her participation ended when she left Georgetown in 1992 to work for the Clinton transition and Administration. Janemarie Mulvey joined The Urban Institute in 1993 and provided crucial help with the project, particularly working on issues regarding Social Security and simulations of out-of-pocket health care spending.

Initial positive prospects for health care reform, for example, seemed to suggest that some of the goals we first set out to espouse would be achieved. But the change in the political environment after the 1994 elections shifted the outlook in the opposite direction. Nonetheless, despite the rhetoric and changing political situation, the basic problems and challenges we identified in 1991 remain today although they are currently somewhat out of vogue. Fortunately, our funders for the project patiently stuck by us. The Retirement Research Foundation generously extended funding several times while we struggled with how to continue the work and shape this book. Additional support from the Henry J. Kaiser Family Foundation permitted updating of analysis in the Medicare and long term care chapters.

We wish to thank a number of people who helped bring this project to completion. Those who read and critiqued our earlier drafts included Linda Blumberg, John Gist, John Sabelhaus, and Timothy Smeeding. Shruti Rajan, Kristen Aleksa, Crystal Kuntz, Saadeh Al-Jurf, and Anuj Shah provided helpful assistance with the programming, and with producing the tables and charts we use.

Marilyn Moon
The Urban Institute
August 1995

Chapter One

THE BIG PICTURE

In 1995, the government of the United States will spend approximately $450 billion on entitlement programs for Americans aged 65 and older—an amount dominated by Social Security and two health care programs, Medicare and Medicaid. Moreover, spending on the elderly under these three programs will constitute about 30 percent of all federal spending in 1995. It is no wonder that those serious about cutting the federal budget have taken on what has sometimes been viewed as sacrosanct territory.

Two of these programs, Social Security and Medicare, are traditionally thought of as "social insurance"—that is, all wage earners contribute to a dedicated tax, and after meeting minimum standards of contributions or other eligibility requirements, they are then assured of benefits.[1] The nearly universal coverage of individuals by these two programs—first as contributors and then as beneficiaries—makes them among the most popular parts of the federal budget. Individuals feel they have a stake in the system and can count on benefits into the future. Furthermore, even when younger persons express doubts about their ultimate receipt of benefits from Social Security or Medicare, they still value the programs highly. This likely reflects the strong ties of many families across generations and a recognition that the young benefit from the security afforded their parents and grandparents. Much of our attention in this volume is directed at these two primary entitlements for the elderly.

Medicaid is also important to older Americans, although it is not a social insurance program as usually defined. It offers health care insurance for people with low incomes. For older Americans, Medicaid is particularly crucial for its coverage of long-term care services. Although the program is not directed exclusively at older Americans, persons aged 65 and older receive a large share of spending on Medicaid. Medicaid is jointly funded with state governments, and the federal government's share comes from general revenues.

A fourth entitlement program, Supplemental Security Income (SSI), provides cash support to low-income elderly persons, but over time it has declined in importance for this age group. Because of the program's small size—only about $6 billion in 1995 for persons aged 65 and above—it does not receive the same emphasis in this volume as the other three public programs (U.S. House 1993).

Entitlement is a budget term that has often taken on a pejorative meaning but which essentially characterizes these programs as not subject to the regular appropriations process, but, rather, as growing in size over time depending upon the impact of requirements for eligibility and benefits as defined by law. Such a budget position offers stability of coverage and predictability of benefits.

Critics of entitlements argue that this protected budget status is undesirable because it is more difficult to change such programs. In 1995, however, it seems that at the least, health care entitlements will be subjected to spending reductions greater than many found elsewhere in the budget. If so, this will mark a major turning point for entitlements and the elderly. Although these programs have been modified in the past, the justification for major policy shifts has tended to be based more on maintaining the long-run solvency of the Social Security and Medicare trust funds. And although Medicare solvency has been tied to the debate since the release of the April 1995 Medicare trustees' report (Board of Trustees, Federal HI Trust Fund 1995), the debate until then centered on major cuts in Medicare and Medicaid specifically for budgetary reasons (Seib 1995).[2]

CHANGING INTEREST IN ENTITLEMENT PROGRAMS

Preparing a study on Social Security, Medicare, and Medicaid is a particularly daunting undertaking at this time. Not only are these large and complicated programs, but each raises a number of politically sensitive issues. And, in 1995, the role of these programs in the future well-being of the elderly seems particularly uncertain. They are likely to wax and wane as political hot potatoes for the next few years.

Early in the 1980s, a trial balloon regarding major cuts in Social Security was floated by President Ronald Reagan's administration and immediately shot down. The popular perception, at least, was that, in 1982, Republicans were soundly punished politically for raising this issue. Nonetheless, in 1983, a historic set of amendments changing both Social Security and Medicare was passed quickly by the U.S. Congress, based on the recommendations of a bipartisan commission established to "save" Social Security. Indeed, the Social Security trust fund had to borrow from the Medicare Hospital Insurance trust fund to avoid failing to meet basic minimum standards while efforts were made to restore balance to the system. The 1983 amendments required sacrifices from taxpayers and beneficiaries alike, and serve as a model of how change can be brought about in the system. It was shown that even the most popular entitlement program, Social Security, can be modified over time—although the changes were not enacted until there was a sense of immediate crisis.

Since then, many efforts to subject these programs to major reform have fallen flat, although smaller-scale alterations in Medicare and Medicaid have taken place. Nearly every year since 1981, for example, the Medicare program has been changed in various ways, either reducing payments to providers of the services that Medicare covers or raising beneficiaries' required contributions. The U.S. Congressional Budget Office (1991) concluded that program changes made in the 1980s reduced spending by 20 percent over what it otherwise would have been. Moreover, these changes pushed back the projected date of insolvency of the Medicare program by over 10 years.

Increasingly, however, proposals to reform these entitlements in the 1990s have been bolder and more dramatic, more often centered on the size of overall government rather than on the long-run status of social insurance programs. For example, former Senator Warren Rudman and former presidential candidate Paul Tsongas have together formed the Concord Coalition, a group that is lobbying for a balanced budget funded to a considerable degree by large reductions in entitlements. Moreover, proposals contained in the health care reform debate of 1994 would have resulted in major changes in Medicare and Medicaid as part of the anticipated overhaul in our health care system. Some of the future financing burden would have been removed from Medicare and Medicaid, essentially by engineering cross-subsidies from required employer contributions into the health care system and by imposing a higher tobacco tax on Americans.

But thus far, major reforms remain proposals, not legislation. For example, a congressionally mandated Bipartisan Commission on Entitlement and Tax Reform (hereafter Entitlement Commission) ended in December 1994 without even majority support for its policy recommendations (Bipartisan Commission on Entitlement and Tax Reform 1995). The commission's charge was to find ways to pare back these programs for the long run in conjunction with possible reductions in tax expenditures.[3] When the two cochairs, Senators Bob Kerrey (D.-Neb.) and John Danforth (R.-Mo.) proposed a set of changes, liberal members of the commission objected to the size of entitlement cuts and conservative members objected to the tax expenditure changes. Consequently, the only agreement the commission could muster was that a problem was looming that needed to be addressed. Because the commission's final report came after the November 1994 congressional election with its historic change in leadership, it is not surprising that the commission captured so little attention. Republican leaders wanted to pursue their own agenda.

The 1994 Social Security Advisory Commission has yet to release its recommendations, and as of spring 1995 it remained divided on what changes to recommend (Rich 1995). Both the Entitlement Commission and the Social Security Advisory Commission focused on the long-range problems facing Social Security and Medicare. These arise essentially as a result of the demographic shifts in the population that will increase the number of people eligible for the programs relative to the numbers paying into the trust funds beginning in about 2010. Although the Social Security program has been building a reserve in its trust funds by raising more in revenues than income in recent years, both Social Security and Medicare are essentially "pay-as-you-go" programs, funding current retirees and disabled beneficiaries with contributions from current workers.[4] Either to move away from such a system or to adjust to the demographic shifts in the ratio of workers to beneficiaries will require substantial changes in these programs. Such an effort will be necessary for the long-range solvency of the system. But these changes will require substantial and painful cures, either in the form of new taxes or lower benefits—medicine that few politicians wish to prescribe.

The likelihood of a more serious discussion of the role of entitlements was, however, elevated when the Congressional Republicans announced they would seek to balance the federal budget by the year 2002. Essentially this added short-run concerns to the longer-run challenges facing these programs. Given the size of entitlements for the elderly, it is nearly mandatory that substantial cuts be made in these programs to achieve the goal of a balanced budget by 2002. Thus, at the least, it would seem that the timetable for cuts in the health entitlement programs has been speeded up substantially. In keeping with that expectation, the congressional budget resolution of June 1995—which set targets for how spending will change in the future—specified $270 billion in cuts in Medicare and $182 billion in Medicaid over a seven-year period. And even though Social Security was presumably exempt from these cuts, substantial savings may be achieved by reducing the amount of the cost-of-living adjustments (COLA) allowed, offered via a "technical" adjustment to the consumer price index (CPI), which serves as the basis for the COLA.

THE FUTURE OF ENTITLEMENTS

Although the 1980s brought some changes in programs for older Americans, we can likely expect many more in the future as the entitlement debate expands. The current budget pressures facing these programs, as well as the more serious longer-term issues accentuated by the aging of the baby boom generation, portend major changes in the future. But how do we begin to think about altering these programs in ways that remain true to legitimate promises? And what changes must be made to improve the targeting of these programs within a constrained budget? The central theme of this volume is the necessity to find a balance between recognizing the need for changes ahead and meeting current promises for benefits.

This volume does not presume to tackle all the issues that must be resolved to deal with the very long-run future of Social Security, Medicare, and Medicaid. Rather, we take a more intermediate view, examining options for beginning an orderly transition to a more targeted approach to social insurance, many of which may need to be enacted in the near term in order to assure a stable program for the next 10 to 15 years.

Not only is it difficult to estimate the impact of policy changes 30 or 40 years into the future, but there are several reasons for approaching reform in stages. First, in the highly partisan atmosphere of current federal policymaking, it will be difficult to achieve an honest dialogue concerning all the options that should be considered. For example, even if new taxation is ruled out as an option eventually, it deserves a fair hearing as part of any long-run solution. The rhetoric of the moment is that tax increases cannot even be discussed.

Further, the future of both Medicare and Medicaid depend substantially on what else happens in the health care system. These programs cannot and should not be walled off from the rest of the health care system. Fundamental restructuring now underway in the private sector will affect the future prospects for Medicare and Medicaid. And if costs continue to rise, some of the solutions will likely need to be systemwide rather than focused just on the public programs. Thus, the ways in which the private health sector changes in the next few years will affect what is possible and desirable for Medicare and Medicaid and will influence what other changes such as higher beneficiary contributions might be required.

Even in the current cost cutting environment, changes to improve these programs—while keeping largely within a constrained budget—should still be considered. To some extent, the great pressures to cut government spending can help to spur some necessary longer-run changes. It makes sense, then, to try to influence policy that is driven by short-run considerations to recognize the longer view as well.

Several themes are developed in the chapters following. First, we argue that it is not necessary to solve all problems in the next few years. Rather, it will be important to begin that process in an orderly fashion with an understanding of what the long-run pressures will likely be. Not all of the changes proposed here are consistent with short-run budget cutting of the sort being debated in 1995, and it is important to recognize where that is the case.

Second, while retaining the principle of social insurance, it is possible to make changes that render Social Security and Medicare more progressive—that is, protecting lower-income seniors while making heavier cuts on those with greater incomes. Much of the growth in well-being of the elderly has occurred at the top of the income distribution, and it is this area where major attention to future changes should be directed. Thus, much of our focus is on the distributional impacts of changes in entitlements on the elderly.

Third, whereas much of this volume focuses on the debate over scaling back entitlements even in the short run, it is important not to automatically assume that everything must be cut. Since one of the important questions about social insurance for senior citizens is whether it could be better targeted to those in need, changes in the program might signal more spending in some areas, while scaling back elsewhere. For example, if Medicare beneficiaries are required to pay a larger share of the costs of their medical care, some expanded protections for those with very low incomes would be in order. Further, crucial gaps in long-term care services ought to be addressed, perhaps funded by changes in Social Security and Medicare. The overall balance of spending must clearly change, but if the programs are to maintain a crucial role in protecting older Americans, the focus should not simply be on cuts. Further, we do not feel constrained to offer savings sufficient to meet the goals outlined in the congressional Budget Resolution for Medicare and Medicaid.

Fourth, we believe that it is vital to view Social Security, Medicare, and Medicaid as a whole rather than treating them as separate entities. Solutions may require changes that might not be made if focusing on only one of these three; in particular, changes that make benefits more progressive need to consider the cumulative effects across all three programs. Too often, the impacts of potential changes in Social Security, Medicare, or Medicaid are treated as though the other programs do not exist. As a consequence, we consider short term changes in Social Security even though it is not scheduled for major budget cuts. Changes in Social Security can be used to moderate the level of change required in Medicare or Medicaid, for example.

Finally, our support for the basic principles of social insurance should not be misunderstood; treating the current system as an inviolable contract and refusing to modify these programs is just as damaging to the programs as overreacting and moving too dramatically to alter them. It is the timing and types of program changes that are at issue and not whether change must occur at all.

Notes

1. Part of Medicare is funded from general revenues and premium contributions. This is discussed in more detail in chapter 5.

2. Each year the trustees of Medicare and Social Security release reports on the solvency of these programs' trust funds. The projected problems for Medicare offered a convenient rationale for cuts already proposed before the report's 1995 release. See chapters 3 and 5 for more discussion of this issue.

3. Tax expenditures refer to deductions or exemptions in the federal personal or corporate income tax. The benefits they provide to individuals or firms may operate much like entitlements, which arise through government spending. They are open-ended in the benefits they offer—not subject to annual appropriations—and their impact on the economy is very similar. Examples of tax expenditures include the home mortgage deduction and the earned income tax credit.

4. A pay-as-you-go system uses current contributions to pay for current benefits, in contrast to a system where individuals' contributions are held over time and then eventually returned in the form of payments based directly on the funds in their accounts. A pay-as-you-go system works well when the ratio of contributors to beneficiaries is either growing or stable. When the number of younger contributors declines substantially as compared to older retirees, then financing becomes a problem. This will happen dramatically when the first of the baby boom generation becomes eligible for Social Security and Medicare benefits shortly before 2010.

Chapter Two

MYTHS ABOUT THE ELDERLY

The public policy debate on entitlements and the elderly is an emotionally charged one with various viewpoints hotly contested. Unfortunately, too often emotions are fueled over "facts" that have little validity. Generalizations about "the elderly" are often true for one portion of that population, but on balance are too sweeping. For example, public opinion reflects myths about the economic status of America's elderly citizens, their reliance on government programs, their tax contributions, and the potential impact of various policy changes. The picture that emerges from an examination of facts on this group is more complicated than is often portrayed by either side of the debate concerning the "worthiness" of senior citizens to be the major beneficiaries of public social programs in the United States.

The old stereotype portrayed the elderly as a group of universally poor individuals, relying mainly upon Social Security. This argument served its promoters well in helping to obtain passage of Medicare and other programs for persons over age 65. But that myth is now being displaced by one that argues that all the elderly are well-off and able to provide for themselves. It also is perpetuated by those with a social agenda, but in this instance the goal is to shrink the role of government. This fits neatly with the view that the federal government's entitlement programs are the major source of needed cuts to balance the federal budget by shortly after the turn of the century. According to proponents of this view, most of the elderly can now fend for themselves, and thus, these programs are becoming outmoded and therefore deserve to be scaled back.

But myths do not serve the goal of good policy, even if they seem expedient for selling a particular viewpoint. The facts have a way of returning to swing the pendulum in the other direction, adding fuel to the opposition. The potential harm from exaggerated claims is substantial, particularly at a time when entitlement programs need a careful reexamination. The demographic pressures in the future will create major challenges that need to be addressed, but the rush to put entitlements on the current budget deficit reduction agenda is also fueled by myths. Whatever the policy outcome, it is better to set the record straight for the coming debate on entitlements. That is the goal of this chapter.

KEY MYTHS CONCERNING ENTITLEMENTS AND THE ELDERLY

The most compelling myths are those with at least some element of truth, but in which the facts are subject to misinterpretation or distortion. The following statements, while not comprising a complete list of myths about the elderly, address key issues for evaluating how programs for the elderly—especially Social Security, Medicare and Medicaid—ought to change over time.

1. *All the elderly are rich.* This statement often follows from observations about general improvements in the economic status of older Americans as compared to 20 or 30 years ago. This myth largely supplants the equally unsubstantiated claim that all the elderly are very poor.
2. *There are no longer any (or many) poor older persons.* This statement often follows from the first myth, and is bolstered by claims that if the dollar values of Medicare and Medicaid are added to the incomes of older persons, very few people would be classified as below the poverty level.
3. *The elderly who do have low incomes are asset rich.* When it is pointed out that many of the elderly do have low incomes, this myth is a counter argument to "prove" statements 1 and 2.
4. *The elderly pay no taxes.* Presumably this statement is true even though they are all rich. Although such an extreme claim is an exaggeration, it is true that tax burdens are lower for older families than for younger ones.
5. *Too much of Social Security goes to wealthy Americans.* If this claim is correct, then enormous savings can be obtained by only cutting back on benefits to the rich. The key question here, however, is how to define who is "rich."
6. *The elderly could do just as well for themselves with private coverage.* Generally this argument accompanies the push to make Social Security voluntary and often assumes that we could shift instantaneously. It is, in fact, a complicated issue in which some

groups are very likely to lose. Here the myth centers more on how painless it would be to shift to a different system.

7. *Public programs are extremely generous and fill in all the gaps in income and health care.* Surely given the dollar amounts of Social Security, Medicaid, and Medicare, it is argued, we have solved any problems facing this group. A slightly different version of this myth is that since these programs are growing so fast, slowing that growth can be done with little effort or sacrifice.

8. *Social Security and Medicare are fully separable programs.* The implication of this myth is that exempting Social Security from changes while focusing cuts on Medicare will satisfy senior citizens. To a lesser extent, there is also a belief that Medicaid is even further removed from these programs.

9. *The social contract with older Americans is a given that cannot and should not be changed.* This claim is often put forth by those seeking to counter some of the preceding myths, but, as indicated by all the changes that have occurred over time and the need for future modifications, it is also a misstatement that may stand in the way of reasonable changes in these programs.

Answers to these myths are combined in the following discussions of the economic status of older Americans, the tax liabilities they face, the contribution of Social Security to economic status, and the adequacy of Medicare and Medicaid to meet the health needs of seniors. The myths that deal more directly with policy must be addressed in the context of the critical trade-offs needed in the future; this is the subject of several of the later chapters in this volume.

ECONOMIC STATUS OF OLDER AMERICANS

By any measure of economic well-being, the circumstances of older Americans have improved substantially over the past three decades. Average incomes and assets for persons over 65 have risen dramatically, from a median per capita income of $3,408 in 1975 to $10,808 in 1993. After controlling for inflation, this represents an 18 percent gain in the purchasing power of this age group.

Why has there been such growth? Income from all sources has risen since early in the 1960s, although pensions and asset income—the sources most associated with private retirement income—have been the most important engines of improvement (Grad 1994). Private pensions have expanded rapidly in recent years, reflecting not only higher awards but also an expanding proportion of retired individuals receiving pensions. Asset incomes may also reflect lump-sum benefits cashed in at retirement. These two sources not only grew in absolute dollars over the past 30 years, but they now consititute a considerably larger share of the pie over time. Together, pensions and asset incomes account for 4 out of every 10 dollars of income for persons aged 65 and older. Over the last 30 years, Social Security benefit increases have also played an important role in income growth, but most of that growth occurred before 1975. Earnings and the "other" category, which includes public assistance, are considerably less important than they were in the 1960s.

But this growth in average income does not mean that all of the elderly are well off or that there are no longer any poor older Americans. To comprehend fully the ability of elderly individuals and families to meet their needs, it is crucial to look beyond these averages and to understand the diversity of groups within the elderly population and in the resources held by them. Income growth has not occurred evenly across the population. Moreover, other indicators of economic status such as poverty and asset holdings also need to be considered. Like so many issues dealing with statistics, it is possible to make many valid, although apparently contradictory, statements.

Diversity and Income

While it is correct to say that the elderly as a group have shown impressive gains, that is not the same as arguing that each elderly individual experienced such gains. If ever it was appropriate to treat persons ages 65 and over as a homogeneous group, it certainly is no longer valid.

Older Americans vary greatly in their financial well-being, depending on their age, ethnic origin, and marital status. For example, as shown in table 2.1, in 1992, elderly black men had per capita median incomes of $7,539, or less than two-thirds the level of their white counterparts. Elderly black single women had the lowest median incomes of all other Americans, averaging just 57 percent of that for the elderly population generally (table 2.1). Moreover, as indicated in the table, median incomes decline steadily with age, leaving the oldest old with lower incomes and less flexibility to adjust their incomes over time for needs such as health care expenses.

Another way to look at the diversity in economic status is to array older persons according to their incomes and see how much difference

Table 2.1 MEDIAN INCOMES FOR VARIOUS GROUPS OF OLDER
AMERICANS, 1992

	All Elderly ($)	Singles ($)	Couples ($)
Age:			
65–69	12,551	11,500	12,884
70–74	11,294	10,651	11,658
75–79	10,426	10,262	10,678
80–84	9,600	9,591	9,609
85 +	9,100	9,152	8,910
Male:			
White	12,118	12,893	12,007
Black	7,539	7,833	7,408
Other	9,585	11,984	8,963
Female:			
White	11,000	10,043	11,901
Black	6,442	6,290	7,308
Other	9,333	7,849	8,458

Source: Current Population Survey, U.S. Bureau of the Census, March 1993.

there is between those at the top and those at the bottom of that
distribution. The average income level for the one-fifth of families
with the highest incomes (the highest quintile) was more than 10
times as high as that for the bottom one-fifth (see table 2.2). The
differences are only slightly less dramatic when comparing singles
and couples separately. Moreover, these incomes are quite low in absolute dollars. It is not until the highest quintile that incomes show a
large increase upward. The highest 20 percent have incomes more
than twice the level of the next-highest 20 percent of families.

Moreover, in recent years the pattern of income growth has increased the dispersion rather than lessened it. Between 1967 and
1979, income growth was disproportionately greater for the lowest

Table 2.2 AVERAGE FAMILY INCOME OF OLDER AMERICANS BY QUINTILE, 1992

Quintile[a]	Singles ($)	Couples ($)	All Elderly Families
First	4,301	9,607	6,272
Second	7,267	17,608	12,493
Third	10,342	24,953	19,607
Fourth	15,051	35,047	30,186
Highest	32,588	75,062	66,829
All	13,900	47,842	40,238

Source: Current Population Survey, U.S. Bureau of the Census, March 1993.
a. Quintiles rank individuals by income from high to low, with each quintile representing one-fifth of all families.

income groups among the elderly, but the opposite has been true since then. For example, between 1979 and 1984, the one-fifth of elderly families with the lowest incomes experienced a decline in real income of $640 on average, compared to a $7,727 increase for elderly families in the top 20 percent between 1979 and 1984 (Radner 1987). And although the changes since then have been less dramatic, the slowest growth in incomes still has occurred for the bottom two quintiles of single elderly persons.[1] Growth has risen the fastest for elderly couples in the highest income quintile. Such families are doing quite well both absolutely and in comparison with younger families. The dichotomy between the wealthiest and the poorest older Americans creates new challenges and belies the notion that we have conquered problems of economic security for this age group.

Poverty

Another way to look at the economic status of older Americans is through measures of poverty. The long-term trend in the poverty rate, which focuses attention on those at the bottom of the income distribution, has declined dramatically for the elderly, again implying that well-being in general for this age group has improved. The share of the elderly in poverty dropped from 28.5 percent in 1966 to a low of 11.4 percent in 1989. In 1982, for the first time, the official rate of poverty among the elderly was lower than that for the rest of the population, and that gap has widened since then (see figure 2.1). The largest declines in poverty rates for the elderly occurred before 1975, however, and the rates have remained relatively flat since 1984 (Moon 1993). By 1992, the poverty rate had again risen to 12.9 percent—above its 1985 level (see table 2.3). For 1993, the rate fell again to 12.4 percent.

Moreover, within the elderly population, poverty rates, like income levels, vary substantially. The most important distinctions are race and persons living alone, particularly women (table 2.4). As table 2.4 indicates, black women between the ages of 80 and 84 have poverty rates approaching 50 percent. Three out of 10 women out of all groups surveyed living alone over the age of 80 are also poor (table 2.4). These statistics are based on the standard poverty definitions used by the U.S. Bureau of the Census, and thus are important for purposes of comparison and consistency with commonly reported data. But measurement issues surrounding these statistics have led to both claims of higher and lower rates of poverty than found in the official numbers.

Figure 2.1 POVERTY RATES BY AGE, 1966 TO 1993

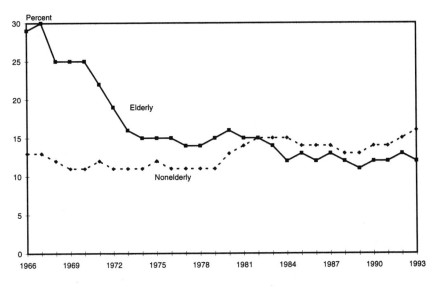

Source: U.S. Congress, House Committee on Ways and Means 1994.

Table 2.3 ELDERLY VERSUS NONELDERLY POVERTY RATES, SELECTED YEARS

	Elderly (%)	Nonelderly (%)
1966	28.5	13.2
1975	15.3	11.8
1980	15.7	12.5
1985	12.6	13.9
1989	11.4	13.0
1992	12.9	14.4

Source: Current Population Reports, Consumer Income Series, P60-185, U.S. Bureau of the Census.

For example, another major government database, the Survey of Income and Program Participation (SIPP), finds both higher incomes and lower rates of poverty among families than does the more commonly used Current Population Survey reported here. Whereas the full range of differences is not well understood, the SIPP interviews families more frequently and is often thought to do a better job of obtaining data on sources that are underreported elsewhere. Thus, if this survey became the standard, rates of poverty would likely fall.

Table 2.4 POVERTY RATES FOR SELECTED GROUPS AMONG THE ELDERLY, 1992

	All	White	Black	Other	Living Alone
Men:					
65–69	9.1	7.3	25.8	27.0	19.7
70–74	7.0	6.0	20.5	3.8	15.9
75–79	8.9	6.8	36.1	34.0	16.1
80–84	11.0	8.7	35.3	23.1	19.1
85+	13.7	10.9	31.4	15.6	18.7
Women:					
65–69	11.5	8.9	32.8	30.4	22.1
70–74	14.1	12.0	36.7	24.3	25.3
75–79	17.0	14.5	44.6	20.7	25.7
80–84	21.7	19.5	47.6	46.7	31.3
85+	22.7	21.9	32.4	48.3	30.2

Source: Current Population Survey, U.S. Bureau of the Census, March 1993.

In addition, poverty numbers have been questioned by researchers who proposed adding the value of noncash benefits, particularly for the Medicare and Medicaid health care programs, to income for purposes of calculating poverty (Smeeding 1984). This approach yields much lower poverty rates, particularly among the elderly, for whom the dollar value of medical benefits is quite high. Such analyses have even prompted some to declare poverty a thing of the past for persons aged 65 and older (Anderson 1978; Hurd 1989; Peterson 1993). But estimating poverty in this way yields the peculiar result that the sicker the demographic group, the better off it will be when medical benefits are counted as income. And as health care costs have risen over the last decade, the problems of using such a measure have become more apparent. Spending for the same benefit package has far outstripped income growth, so that if nothing else changed, it would still appear that fewer elderly persons are in poverty each year. For example, under some of the valuation methods formerly used by the Census Bureau, it was impossible for a single person over age 75 to be poor at all, because the insurance value of Medicare was greater than the poverty income threshold (U.S. Bureau of the Census [henceforth, Census Bureau] 1990). Using those methods, a very elderly homeless person who had no cash income but who was eligible for Medicare still would not be counted as poor—certainly a nonsensical result.

In recent years considerable criticism of this approach has led to a modification in how noncash benefits should be incorporated in poverty measures and further proposals for change.[2] Such proposals may actually lead to an *increase* in the estimated number of poor seniors, once medical care spending is taken into account. This occurs because even with Medicare coverage, many seniors have substantial out-of-pocket liabilities for health care. For example, recent work by Weinberg and Lamas (1993) offered two alternative approaches to poverty measurement, both of which would increase the poverty rate among the elderly. Using 1989 data, they suggested that instead of 12.8 percent, the poverty rates could be as high as 14.7 percent or 20.1 percent. In this same study, poverty rates jumped by 10 percentage points for persons in families with female householders and no spouse present.

Another analysis of poverty measurement suggests other reasons why poverty rates may be understated overall, with figures for the elderly particularly misleading (Ruggles 1990). First, the official estimates use lower poverty lines for one- and two-person households with heads over age 65 as compared to those under age 65, even though those distinctions now make little sense in terms of the consumption patterns and needs of the elderly. Simply eliminating this distinction would result in a substantial increase in the elderly poverty rate. Using this approach for 1992, the percentage would rise from 12.9 percent to 15.4 percent, above that for the overall population. And for women living alone, the percentages would increase from 22.8 to 31.6 percent (see table 2.5).

Further, the measures of poverty we use for all persons have lagged behind the growth in our living standards in general. Updating these measures would again result in more persons being classified as poor, with a disproportionate increase in the number of elderly designated as poor. Under these alternatives, the poverty rate for the elderly would again be higher than the rate for the population as a whole, and would approach the poverty rates for the elderly seen in the mid-1960s. If both of these changes were made in the poverty thresholds, Ruggles (1990) argued that almost one-third of those aged 65 or more would be counted as poor. Ruggles estimated that the thresholds would rise about 25 percent if recalibrated—an amount that would substantially increase the number of people counted as poor.

Poverty rates for the elderly are particularly sensitive to the level of the poverty thresholds used, because a very large number of older persons have incomes just above the official poverty lines. In 1992, 4.0 million individuals 65 or older were counted as poor under the official measure, but another 2.3 million had incomes of no more than 25 percent above the poverty threshold. And if the cutoff for being counted as poor were raised to 150 percent of the official poverty threshold, 27.6 percent of the elderly—about 8.5 million people—

Table 2.5 SELECTED POVERTY RATES, USING ALTERNATIVE POVERTY INCOME
THRESHOLD DEFINITIONS, 1992

	Elderly Poverty Rate (%)		Alternative Measure (%)[a]	
	< 100%	< 125%	< 100%	< 125%
All Elderly	12.9	20.4	15.4	23.7
Males	8.9	14.5	10.65	17.2
Females	15.7	24.5	18.7	28.2
Age:				
65–69	10.4	15.6	12.0	17.9
70–74	10.9	18.0	13.2	21.3
75–79	13.7	22.0	16.8	26.1
80–84	17.6	27.1	20.5	31.6
85 +	19.7	32.77	24.5	36.2
Living Alone:	19.2	29.4	27.2	43.0
Male	12.3	19.6	20.4	33.2
Female	22.8	34.0	31.6	45.6
Race:				
White	10.9	18.0	13.2	21.1
Black	33.3	45.3	37.0	48.6
Other	14.6	22.3	19.0	30.8

Source: Current Population Survey, U.S. Bureau of the Census, March 1993.
a. The alternative measures apply the nonelderly poverty threshold to the elderly.

would have been counted as poor (Census Bureau 1993b). A large
portion of the elderly remain in the near-poor category; they have not
"escaped" very far above the poverty level. If poverty thresholds were
increased for persons of all ages, the share of the elderly in poverty
would thus rise faster than for other groups. At 150 percent of poverty,
23.6 percent of the under-age-65 population would be poor, compared
to 27.6 percent of those over 65. And while the share of elderly in
poverty would still be below that for children (32.8 percent), the percentages are much closer together than when looking at the formal
poverty thresholds. And if the elderly are judged on a standard equivalent to that for the young, the numbers would be even more dramatic.

As shown in table 2.5, the poverty rates for all elderly persons would
rise from 12.9 percent (if the traditional measure is used) to 23.7
percent (when poverty is measured at 1.25 times the nonelderly
threshold).[3] Various subgroups of the elderly show similar dramatic
differences in reported poverty rates. Over one-third of those ages 85
and above would be poor by the 125 percent of the nonelderly threshold measure, and, using the same measure, more than two-fifths of
those living alone would be classified as poor.

Poverty statistics are thus an area where the gains made by seniors and their status compared to other groups may well be misinterpreted.[4] Poverty has not been eliminated; in actuality, it is likely to be substantially higher than reported in the official statistics, since most of the adjustments needed to improve the measure would shift the share of elderly persons in poverty upward.

Assets

Another element of economic well-being, wealth, is generally reflected in the asset incomes of the elderly. Particularly for higher-income families, this represents an important source of income. But assets have advantages in addition to the income they generate; control over a stock of resources and the implicit advantages of, for example, owning one's own home also enhance well-being. Homeownership generally reduces necessary spending on shelter, particularly for those who have paid off their mortgages. Persons can deplete their assets to supplement their incomes, either formally by purchasing annuities or informally by dipping into these reserves to meet their needs. Even when assets are not drawn down in this way, they represent a type of insurance to older persons against unusual expenses.[5]

One response by casual observers to the modest incomes of the elderly is that they may be income poor but asset rich. This claim is considerably exaggerated, however. Homeownership is widespread among the elderly—even a majority of those in the bottom income quintile are homeowners, for example. But, most of the elderly who have substantial assets—particularly financial assets—also have substantial incomes. Older persons with modest means are likely to hold much of their wealth in housing—an asset that is difficult to liquidate to meet short-term needs and may carry substantial burdens in the form of high taxes or maintenance costs as well. Financial assets, which can be readily used to meet short-term needs, are very unequally distributed across the elderly population.

In 1991, the median value of financial assets (i.e., net worth excluding home equity) for the elderly with incomes in the highest 20 percent of the income distribution was almost $300,000, but was only about $3,600 for elderly households in the bottom fifth of the income distribution (1993).[6] A more detailed accounting of the 1991 relationship between assets and income is shown in table 2.6.[7] For persons in the top two quintiles, both financial and total net worth are very high. Age patterns are also interesting; whereas median assets decline

Table 2.6 MEDIAN NET WORTH, BY AGE OF HOUSEHOLDER AND HOUSEHOLD INCOME QUINTILE, 1991

Household Income	Total All Households	Total Ages 65 and Above	Ages 65 to 69 Years	Ages 70 to 74 Years	Ages 75 and Above
All Households (thousands)	94,692	20,638	6,435	5,439	8,764
Median Net Worth	$36,623	$88,192	$104,354	$92,793	$76,541
Excluding Home Equity	10,263	26,442	33,345	25,943	22,866
Net Worth by Income Quintile[a]					
Lowest Quintile:					
Households (thousands)	18,977	7,226	1,657	1,630	3,939
Median net worth	$5,224	$32,172	$30,622	$31,825	$32,946
Excluding home equity	1,143	3,577	2,570	3,083	4,570
Second Quintile:					
Households (thousands)	18,912	5,860	1,760	1,526	2,574
Median net worth	$19,191	$90,635	$92,321	$89,306	$89,975
Excluding home equity	5,588	29,152	25,690	25,808	34,492
Third Quintile:					
Households (thousands)	18,969	3,523	1,306	1,141	1,075
Median net worth	$28,859	$154,203	$154,487	$140,226	$171,032
Excluding home equity	8,661	68,372	64,164	64,280	83,472
Fourth Quintile:					
Households (thousands)	18,928	2,279	968	657	654
Median net worth	$49,204	$225,594	$201,867	$212,062	$303,510
Excluding home equity	16,352	121,154	83,101	123,268	181,513
Highest Quintile:					
Households (thousands)	18,905	1,751	744	485	522
Median net worth	$123,166	$424,721	$382,551	$433,049	$485,557
Excluding home equity	48,893	299,679	226,894	315,194	399,301

Source: Survey of Income and Program Participation.
a. Quintile upper limits: lowest quintile—$12,852; second—$22,944; third—$34,968; fourth—$53,448.

for the whole age group, when controlling by income, asset holdings actually increase with age.

Not shown in table 2.6 are the discrepancies by characteristics such as sex and marital status. These variations are similar to those found in incomes of the elderly. In addition, when compared to 1988 data, the 1991 net worth data represent a substantial improvement for those in the top 20 percent, but a decline for elderly families with the lowest incomes. Thus, even if assets are taken into account in measuring well-being, relatively few of today's low-income elderly would be counted as well off. At the same time, table 2.6 indicates that older Americans are more likely to have financial assets as compared to younger families, indicating that a full accounting of well-being should recognize this source for older persons.[8] Such an adjustment would further underscore the diversity of well-being within the elderly.

The Future

The future economic status of the elderly will depend on many unknown factors. Life expectancy, health status, age of retirement, savings behavior, the overall health of the economy, and public policy changes will all play a role. If the trends of the last decade were simply taken as projections into the next, we would expect to see continued steady growth in average incomes of the elderly, continued improvement relative to the working population, and a general trend toward somewhat lower poverty rates. In turn, we could also expect higher levels of assets and less reliance on relatives.

Evidence from the 1950–80 Censuses (Ross, Danziger, and Smolensky 1989) and from wealth surveys taken between 1962 and 1984 (Wolff 1987) indicate that the next generation of elderly (i.e., those born between 1920 and 1935, and reaching age 65 between 1985 and 2000) will be considerably better off as they age than their older counterparts. This age group (aged 25–40 in 1960) had the good fortune to be in their prime working years during the period of maximum earnings growth of the halcyon 1960s, to find the value of their homes soaring during the inflation of the 1970s, and to be in the maximum liquid asset position to capture most fully the benefits of high real interest rates and the stock market boom of the early to mid-1980s. This group may also prove to be better off than cohorts that follow after the turn of the century.

There are several reasons for caution in assuming ever-rising increases in economic status for the elderly. First, the growth rate of

Social Security benefits is likely to slow in the future. Low rates of inflation and slow wage growth in the 1980s and now in the 1990s will carry over into Social Security benefits that new retirees will receive. And low inflation rates mean lower cost of living increases for existing recipients. The ad hoc increases in Social Security benefits that helped raise living standards in the 1950s through 1970s no longer boost this income source in inflation-adjusted terms.

Second, income from private pensions, which has shown rapid growth in recent years, is leveling off. Growth in coverage by private pensions is also expected to move at a slower pace, since much of the growth in employment in the United States is now in the service sector, an area where fringe benefits tend to be less generous on average than in manufacturing (Wiatroski 1993; Zedlewski et al. 1990). Corporate downsizing and other adjustments to slower economic growth do not bode well for retirement benefits in the future. Both the level of benefits as a share of income and the number of persons receiving them are unlikely to grow by much.

Third, the changing age composition of the elderly—with more of the oldest old than ever before—will also reduce the extent to which incomes grow over time. These factors will not necessarily be equally felt across the elderly population. In the 1990s, growth in the numbers of persons 65 and over will be concentrated in the over-age-85 category, reflecting increased life expectancies. Individuals reaching retirement age will have been born in the 1930s, a period when birthrates were very low. For example, between 1990 and the year 2000, the population between the ages of 65 and 74 will grow by only 1.2 percent, while the age 85 and above group will grow by 34 percent (U.S. House 1992). Thus, the very old will grow as a proportion of the elderly, and their lower average incomes are likely to help hold down overall rates of growth in income as compared to the 1970s. These oldest Americans are least likely to work, and their pension, Social Security, and other incomes are unlikely to increase markedly over time. At best, they will keep pace with inflation. It is people newly turning age 65 who tend to raise average incomes over time.

These changes also suggest that the disparity in incomes within the elderly is likely to increase, as has been the trend for some time. If Social Security becomes less important as a source of income and if life expectancies continue to rise, for example, the status of the oldest old, who largely depend on Social Security benefits, will lag further behind that of other elderly families whose sources of income (such as from assets) continue to grow. Moreover, current public policy suggests that programs aiding those with lower incomes are unlikely to expand. Perhaps most important, a long trend since the mid-1970s toward increasing inequality in younger families suggests a pattern that is likely to carry over to the elderly for the indefinite future. The findings of greater concentration in wealth holdings reported previously also raise questions about inequality in this source of economic status, underscoring inequality in total well-being.

Another important unknown in how we view the well-being of the elderly is their status relative to other groups. Although predicting growth for the elderly is difficult in and of itself, it is even harder to predict how such growth will compare with income changes for younger working families. If the trends discussed here hold and the economy experiences relatively rapid real growth in the next decade, the status of the elderly relative to the young could again decline. It is more likely, however, that the economic position of the elderly will stabilize relative to that of their younger counterparts for the time being. This relative status of the elderly will be important in any political debates over what should happen to entitlements, since many of the potential policy alternatives involve trade-offs between burdens on the old and the young.

Summarizing the Economic Status of the Elderly

How should we compile all this information to describe the economic status of seniors? Different data are relevant depending upon the question under consideration.

For example, consider the issue of increases in economic status over time. Do we mean progress for the elderly as one large group or for specific individuals? Some of the increase in well-being attributed to the elderly across time reflects the changing composition of the elderly population. Each year individuals turning age 65 join the elderly "category," and the incomes of these newly elderly individuals have tended on average to be higher with each succeeding year. At the same time, some of the oldest old, who have lower incomes on average, die. Thus, even if there were no real (inflation-adjusted) growth in the income of any specific elderly individual each year, these demographic changes would yield steady improvements in reported average income levels (Moon 1987). But individuals within the elderly population display much slower rates of income growth than does the group as a whole. For example, between 1982 and 1992, the rates of poverty for all women aged 65 and over declined from 17.5 to 15.7 percent. But if we look at a specific cohort—for example, women aged

65 to 72 in 1982 and 75 to 82 in 1992, their poverty rates actually grew from 14.4 percent to 18.8 percent (Census Bureau 1984; 1993b).

Another critical issue is that of defining what is meant by "high income" or "rich" elderly persons. These terms are frequently used in proposals to means test or cut back benefits for certain groups of the elderly. Ironically, a double standard seems to be at work. For example, one set of proposals that has received considerable attention suggested phasing out Social Security, Medicare, and all other government benefits for those with incomes above $40,000 per year (Peterson 1993). But in the 1993 debate over federal income tax changes, some of these same policymakers claimed that the middle class extended up to $100,000 or $200,000 of income (Starobin 1994). And the tax cuts proposed in 1995 by Republicans in the U.S. House of Representatives also set $200,000 as the middle-income "standard." Particularly for older Americans, such distinctions are critical. Should we have different criteria for some programs than for others? That is, should the definition of middle class be different between young families and those over age 65? And if so, how much different? Choosing the appropriate absolute level will always require a subjective decision, but it is reasonable either to set a consistent standard among age and other groups, or to develop reasonable ways of establishing equivalence. Similarly, it makes sense to use consistent definitions for "rich" or "middle-class" families for policies affecting government benefits and taxes.

Overall, the outlook appears to be good for most of the elderly, although future improvements are likely to come at a slower pace than in recent years. Nonetheless, a substantial minority of the elderly will still have incomes that are at best barely adequate to meet their needs. The diversity of needs within this population subgroup will prove a major source of contention in further policy debates. It is always easier to treat this group homogeneously; policies that begin to further subdivide the elderly raise political and practical challenges.

TAX LIABILITIES

Older Americans have long received preferential treatment through the income tax, although not nearly to the extent sometimes claimed in the popular press. The elderly have lower tax burdens relative to the young, but to a considerable degree this is because they have lower incomes on average. In 1992, the median income for all elderly households was $17,160, nearly half of the $35,639 median income reported for nonelderly households (Census Bureau 1993a). Lower incomes for the elderly reflect fewer wage earners and smaller families, and to the extent that this explains lower tax liabilities, there is no basis for concern. But a substantial share of the income of moderately well-off elderly families comes from Social Security, which traditionally was not taxed (although that has changed substantially in recent years). This also helps explain differences in tax liabilities.

To get a sense of the relative importance of each effect, consider two examples shown in table 2.7. First, in the top panel of the table, tax liabilities are calculated for elderly and nonelderly couples with incomes at the median. This example represents a combination of the exclusion of Social Security from taxes as well as the effect of income differences between the elderly and nonelderly. In this example, the average income tax rate for the nonelderly family (assuming no item-ization or deductions) would be nearly 10 times higher than that for

Table 2.7 TAX LIABILITY OF ELDERLY VERSUS NONELDERLY COUPLES

	Elderly	Nonelderly
Tax Calculation for Median Elderly and Nonelderly Couple		
Total Income:	$25,448	$45,000
Social Security benefits	−$11,496	—
Adjusted Gross Income:	$13,952	$45,000
Exemptions	−$4,600	−$4,600
Standard deductions	−$7,400	−$6,000
Taxable Income	$1,952	$34,400
Taxes Owed	$294	$5,164
Average Tax Rate	1.15%	11.5%
Tax Calculation When Sources of Income Are Equal		
Total Income:	$40,000	$40,000
Social Security benefits	−$10,370	—
Adjusted Gross Income:	$29,630	$40,000
Exemptions	−$4,600	−$4,600
Standard deductions	−$7,400	−$6,000
Taxable Income	$17,630	$29,400
Taxes Owed	$2,664	$4,414
Average Tax Rate	6.6%	11.0%

Source: Authors' calculations for hypothetical couples.

the elderly couple. The second example (in the bottom panel of the table) displays elderly and nonelderly couples with equal incomes. Thus, the difference is wholly attributable to the exclusion of some Social Security from taxation. In this example, the elderly couple's taxes are 40 percent lower than those of the nonelderly because of the preferential treatment of Social Security. Exempting part of Social Security from taxation is usually justified on the grounds that workers pay tax on their contributions to the program.

The exclusion of Social Security and other income from taxation does raise issues about preferential treatment for the elderly. Prior to 1980, a large portion of nonwage income sources were excluded from taxation. Since then, a number of provisions in the tax code that were favorable to the elderly have been eliminated or modified, thus raising their taxable income. These provisions include: (1) taxation of some Social Security benefits, (2) elimination of the extra personal exemption for the aged, (3) changes in the treatment of capital gains, and (4) limitations on the deductibility of medical expenses. As a result of changes in the preferential treatment of these sources, elderly tax burdens have risen over the past decade, but still remain well below the tax burdens of the nonelderly (see table 2.8). Changes in the tax code during the 1980s can be categorized into two main areas: increased taxation of nonwage income (primarily Social Security) and the elimination of certain tax preferences that affected both the elderly and nonelderly.

The 1983 Social Security Amendments required higher-income beneficiaries to report half of their Social Security benefits as part of taxable income. This substantially increased income taxes for single persons with incomes over $25,000 per year and couples with incomes over $32,000. Individuals with income below the thresholds are required to pay taxes on up to 50 percent of their Social Security benefits. As a result of these changes, overall income tax liabilities

Table 2.8 TOTAL EFFECTIVE FEDERAL TAX RATES, BY FAMILY TYPE, 1977–92

Family Type	1977 (%)	1980 (%)	1985 (%)	1988 (%)	1992 (%)
All Families	22.8	23.3	21.7	22.9	23.3
All Elderly:	16.5	16.8	14.7	16.2	16.3
Couples	16.9	17.4	14.7	16.9	17.2
Singles	13.9	14.1	11.9	13.7	13.7
Other	18.4	18.4	17.5	17.5	17.4
All Nonelderly	23.8	24.4	23.1	24.2	24.7

Source: Sammartino and Williams (1991).

for Social Security benefits rose by $2.3 billion in 1984 (the first year of taxation), and by 1992 totaled about $6.2 billion (U.S. House 1994). Moreover, the number of elderly beneficiaries affected by this taxation has risen steadily over time and is expected to reach 22.9 percent by 1995. The budget agreement of 1993 raised these tax amounts further by creating a second tier of taxation that raised the taxable share to 85 percent for couples with incomes over $44,000 and for singles with incomes over $34,000. Whereas earlier revenues from taxation went directly to the Old-Age and Survivors Insurance (OASI) trust fund, these additional revenues from the 1993 legislation were allocated to the Medicare Hospital Insurance (HI) trust fund.

In addition to the tax treatment of Social Security, many tax preferences affecting both the elderly and nonelderly were eliminated through the Tax Reform Act of 1986 (TRA), changes that were believed to reduce much of the complexity in the tax code. Further, by broadening the base of taxable income, marginal tax rates were allowed to fall to achieve a similar stream of tax revenues as before. The tax structure was also simplified from 14 tax brackets ranging from 11 percent to 50 percent to only 2 brackets of 15 percent and 28 percent.

A number of provisions of the Tax Reform Act of 1986 directly affected the elderly. Prior to tax reform, taxpayers over age 65 were able to take an extra personal exemption. In 1985, this exemption was worth $1,080. Under the TRA, this exemption was eliminated and was replaced by an additional standard deduction for the elderly of $2,480 for singles and $3,670 for married couples. This change from an allowable exemption to a standardized deduction benefits only those elderly who do not itemize because they are the only ones eligible for a standard deduction. Thus, this tax change would disproportionately affect higher-income elderly persons. As a result of these changes, the elderly who previously itemized—estimated to be about one-third of taxpayers in 1985 (Zedlewski 1988)—experienced an increase in their taxable income.

Tax reform also changed the amount of medical expenses that can be deducted from taxable income. Prior to 1986, individuals were able to deduct medical expenses that exceeded 5 percent of adjusted gross income. Tax reform increased the threshold for deducting medical expenses from 5 percent to 7.5 percent of adjusted gross income. A change in this threshold largely affects the elderly, who typically experience substantially higher out-of-pocket health expenditures compared to the nonelderly. For example, projections for 1994 indicate that the elderly currently spend 21 percent of their income on health care services (American Association of Retired Persons 1994).

A third provision that disproportionately affected the elderly was the elimination of the capital gains exclusion. Prior to 1986, up to 60 percent of capital gains were excluded from taxable income. The Tax Reform Act of 1986 eliminated special treatment of capital gains, thus making all capital gains subject to taxation at the same tax rate that personal income is taxed.[9] Because the elderly have a larger share of capital gains, this provision disproportionately affects them, raising their effective tax rates. Among the elderly, this provision most likely affects those in the upper-income brackets who have a larger share of capital gains. There were many other miscellaneous provisions of the TRA that affected both the elderly and nonelderly. These included the elimination of the two-earner deduction, curtailment of deductions for travel and entertainment expenses, limitations of individual retirement account (IRA) contributions, and elimination of the $100/$200 dividend exclusion.

A study by Zedlewski (1988) using The Urban Institute's TRIM model examined the effect of the Tax Reform Act of 1986 on both the elderly and nonelderly and found that older Americans paid $739 million more in federal income taxes as a result of tax reform. However, this cost was borne largely by taxpayers in the upper-income brackets. In contrast, younger taxpayers paid $22 billion less (about 8 percent) owing to tax reform.

Thus, whereas older Americans still pay lower taxes on average as compared to younger persons, this situation has changed considerably over the last decade. Much of the difference in taxes stems from the low share of wages in seniors' incomes, reducing both their income and payroll tax liabilities compared to those of younger families. While policy changes over the past 15 years have alleviated much of the preferential treatment for the elderly in the tax code, legislation proposed by the House of Representatives in 1995 attempts to roll back the Social Security tax and reinstitute a capital gains exclusion. The passage of this legislation would reverse much of the progress in making the tax code more equitable across generations.

CONTRIBUTION OF SOCIAL SECURITY

The impact of Social Security on the income of older Americans represents a critical measure of the importance of the program. Social Security payments constitute the largest source of income for Americans over the age of 65, accounting for about 36 percent of their total income. But various groups differ in terms of who benefits. Social Security as a share of income is much larger for the poor and near-poor, minorities, and the old-old. For example, the two-fifths of elderly families with the lowest incomes rely on Social Security for nearly 75 percent of their incomes (see table 2.9). Minorities and the old-old (aged 85 plus) also rely more heavily on Social Security (see table 2.10).

To further highlight the importance of Social Security benefits on the overall well-being of the elderly, consider the distribution of this age group by income class with and without Social Security benefits.

Table 2.9 SHARES OF AGGREGATE INCOME OF ELDERLY BY TOTAL INCOME QUINTILE, 1992

Percentage of Income from:	Quintile					
	1st	2nd	3rd	4th	5th	Total
Social Security	72.7	72.8	58.2	39.2	19.4	46.6
Any pension	3.3	71	15.5	21.6	19.1	15.6
Earnings	1.8	7.1	12.0	20.5	37.7	19.3
Income from assets	5.8	5.3	8.7	14.7	19.4	12.3
Public assistance	10.4	4.2	1.3	0.6	0.2	2.1
Other	4.2	3.3	4.3	3.6	4.2	3.9

Source: Urban Institute tabulations from 1992 Current Population Survey, U.S. Bureau of the Census.

Table 2.10 SHARES OF INCOME FOR ELDERLY

	Age 65 +			Age 85 +		
	White	Black	Hispanic	White	Black	Hispanic
Married:						
Social Security	56.8	65.5	61.0	60.9	68.3	82.7
Pensions	15.3	11.1	10.9	10.3	10.5	11.1
Earnings	7.4	7.8	7.8	1.6	9.5	0.0
Assets	17.1	4.7	8.3	24.2	4.3	0.1
Other	2.8	8.0	9.6	3.0	7.4	6.1
Unmarried:						
Social Security	63.5	69.1	58.0	68.1	73.0	54.8
Pensions	9.2	6.5	4.8	6.8	4.0	0.3
Earnings	3.0	6.0	5.4	0.7	0.5	0.0
Assets	14.2	2.5	3.0	14.7	2.2	5.9
Other	9.4	15.0	20.8	8.7	20.3	36.8

Source: Urban Institute tabulations from 1992 Current Population Survey, U.S. Bureau of the Census.

If Social Security benefits were subtracted from family income, nearly 51 percent of the elderly would become impoverished (i.e., income below $6,000 in 1990) (Grad 1994). This is in sharp contrast to the 10.7 percent of the elderly who are currently impoverished even with the inclusion of Social Security benefits as income. Put another way, over 50 percent of the elderly population with Social Security benefits have a family income of less than $20,000. Without Social Security, nearly 80 percent of the elderly have family incomes below $20,000 (Grad 1994).

Thus, for these groups Social Security plays an essential role. But could Social Security do better by reducing payments to higher-income beneficiaries or by privatizing the program, as many suggest?

Social Security and Higher-Income Beneficiaries

Despite Social Security's success in aiding people with low and moderate incomes, there is a growing belief that too much of Social Security is directed at wealthier families. Proponents of scaling back the program often argue that most of it goes to those who are already quite well off. However, the issue is considerably more complicated. First, it is important to define who is "well off." Does this include middle-class families for example? And does middle class mean $100,000 of income or more, as some have suggested? The middle class is typically defined as containing individuals who have income near the median of a given group. At the median income level, 50 percent of individuals fall above this level and 50 percent fall below. In 1992, the median income for elderly households was $17,160—or only about twice the poverty threshold. If we expand the notion of middle class to include the third and fourth quintiles of the income distribution—capturing 40 percent of families—the income range would be $15,659 to $37,827 in 1992 dollars. Such elderly families and individuals do receive above-average benefits, such that this 40 percent of the population accounts for about 48 percent of all Social Security benefits paid to persons aged 65 and over. But it is hard to argue that these families and individuals have high incomes.

If, instead, we look only at those in the top quintile, where incomes average $66,829, the importance of Social Security benefits declines substantially as a share of income to less than 19 percent (table 2.9). The average dollar value of such benefits is relatively high, however. Limiting benefits to these families would thus generate substantial savings, but it is hard to argue that such families are "wealthy." And moving higher up the income scale would affect even fewer families.

Privatization as a Solution

Past retirees have received or are receiving benefits far greater than the value of the taxes they paid, and future retirees are expected to face declining and in some cases negative rates of return on Social Security. For example, single males with average earnings retiring in 1970 will have a real lifetime internal rate of return of 6.37 percent. For those retiring in 2010, their rate of return is expected to decline to 1.16 percent (Steuerle and Bakija 1994).

These differences have prompted some to recommend that individuals would be better off if Social Security were changed to a program whereby individuals save on their own in private accounts. Would the rates of return to Social Security contributors increase if Social Security were privatized? Privatization proposals, although gaining popularity over the past decade, will not necessarily raise the rates of return substantially. In fact, such proposals carry considerable uncertainty regarding their outcomes, for a number of reasons.

First, Social Security's lower expected returns over time are due not to public investment of the trust fund balances; rather, they are a result of changing demographics in the United States, which will be reflected in an expected reduction in worker-to-retiree ratios as baby boomers retire. There will simply be fewer persons contributing payroll tax revenues to fund benefit payments. This demographic shift will require either a reduction in benefits or an increase in the contribution from workers to keep the system solvent. Privatization would have to achieve enormous gains to overcome this demographic problem.

Second, any search for higher returns is essentially a search for investments that pay higher returns—and by definition are riskier. One of the first issues that should always be examined in any proposal for private investment of resources that would otherwise go into the Social Security program is the trade-off between return and protection of the principal. Social Security represents the most secure of all forms of retirement savings. Its funds are conservatively invested in government securities, and there is an implicit promise of the full faith and resources of the federal government backing up these funds. This provides individuals with the assurance that they can take more risk with private investments either through their own 401k and other plans or through fully private savings.

Finally, one of the major problems with privatization is transition costs. Social Security is basically a pay-as-you-go system. Current workers pay for current retirees and in return they expect to receive benefits in the future that will be funded by future workers. To maintain fairness, a major restructuring of Social Security would still have to pay benefits to current beneficiaries for some time period to fulfill the original promise of the program. Such a transition could be costly and result in lower rates of return during the transition for those who must contribute for their own benefits and to pay for the phase-out of the existing program.

The Social Security program is not and should not simply be thought of as a pension system. It has many other goals that take priority over a simple calculation of the benefits that can be achieved compared to benefits paid in. First, it is a program intended to offer a floor of protection for qualifying Americans. This means that some redistribution must occur, paying higher benefits relative to contributions for those with the lowest resources. In addition, Social Security offers disability and survivor protections that also need to be funded before considering giving individuals more flexibility over their own contributions.

It might be possible to achieve higher returns through privatization, but the complexities and uncertainties associated with such a major change need careful scrutiny. The serious attention being given to such proposals suggests, however, that they may well become part of a long-run strategy for change. Clearly, the practical concerns raised here need to be explored further before such major reform is undertaken.

ADEQUACY OF MEDICARE AND MEDICAID

Another continuing challenge to the well-being of older Americans is the burden of health care spending by individuals. Despite the introduction of Medicare (for the elderly) and Medicaid (for those with low incomes) in 1965, the percentage of income spent on out-of-pocket, unreimbursed health care costs by persons over age 65 is at an all-time high and is projected to increase further (Moon 1993). Incomes have risen for this age group, but out-of-pocket health costs have simply risen faster. At the same time, overall spending on Medicare and Medicaid has also increased sharply. Both the government and individuals are feeling the pinch of higher health care spending.

Analyses of the acute-care portion of these expenses reveal considerable burdens on those with low or moderate incomes. We have estimated that by 1994, spending on acute-care out-of-pocket services and premiums averaged 21 percent of the incomes of *all* the elderly, and if we look at average out-of-pocket burdens for the poor and persons over the age of 80, the percentages rise to 30 percent or more (see table 2.11). Premiums are lower as a share of income for higher-income persons both because they pay the same dollar premium for Medicare as those with lower incomes and because they are more likely to receive subsidized premiums for supplemental coverage as part of their retirement benefits. This also factors into the age differences shown in table 2.11. Younger households are considerably more likely to have retirement benefits, as well as higher incomes. Very low-income families are eligible for special protections under Medicaid, but the overall shares are still high because of low participation.[10]

How much of this growth simply reflects older persons' desires to finance health care spending rather than other consumption activities? Certainly some growth in spending over time reflects such desires working in concert with incentives for consuming more health care because of the subsidies that insurance provides. And to the extent that these changes are discretionary, they may not be viewed as fully reducing standards of living for the elderly. On the other hand,

Table 2.11 HEALTH CARE SPENDING OUT-OF-POCKET AND ON PREMIUMS AS SHARE OF INCOME

| | Percentage of Elderly | Per Capita Spending ($) | | Health Expenditure as Share of Family Income (%)[a] |
		Out-of-Pocket	Insurance Premiums	
Poverty Status:				
Under 100%	12.1	913	653	34
100–125%	8.0	1,047	1,069	27
125–200%	20.5	1,456	1,268	26
200–400%	35.1	1,486	1,200	18
Over 400%	24.4	1,509	1,199	13
Age:				
65–69	33.7	972	1,078	18
70–74	26.5	1,121	1,143	19
75–79	19.9	1,357	1,231	20
80–84	11.5	2,296	1,193	31
85+	8.4	2,700	1,082	29
Total	—	1,382	1,137	21

Source: Authors' simulations using NMES (National Medical Expenditure Survey).
a. Although the dollars shown in this table are per capita, the shares of income are estimated by family, recognizing that it is family budgets and combined spending that matter.

the rate of growth in spending by Medicare (which is closely linked to the rate of growth of out-of-pocket spending) has been equal to or below that for younger privately insured persons for at least a decade. New technology and high rates of health care inflation are also major keys to growth in spending.

As serious as these considerations are, the costs of long-term care hold the potential for even more devastating reductions in economic status for older families. An individual may pay, on average, $30,000 to $35,000 for a year's stay in a nursing home. Medicare pays virtually nothing of these costs, and Medicaid will only cover these costs once an individual has spent down nearly all of his or her assets. Eventually, Medicaid pays about half of the costs of nursing home services and a much smaller share of care in the home.[11] Moreover, people with disabilities are also more likely to incur acute-care expenses, increasing further their overall burdens. In fact, the share of income spent on acute care by those with two or more limitations in activities of daily living (a standard measure of disability) was three times as high as for the elderly population as a whole (Drabek and Moyer 1994). Thus, even with the protections added in recent years, the spouse remaining in the community will likely be placed in severely straightened circumstances. Consequently, even middle-class families can find it impossible to meet their health care needs.

The likelihood of incurring costs from both acute- and long-term health care needs rises steadily with age—in reverse proportion to ability to pay. That is, it is the elderly woman living alone who is most at risk of needing long-term care services (Doty, Liu, and Wiener 1985). And the outlook for the future is not particularly reassuring. Wiener, Illston, and Hanley (1994) suggested that only a minority of older families will ever be able to afford to protect themselves against long-term care expenditures.

Thus, whereas Medicare and Medicaid expenditures for the elderly have grown rapidly since their inception in 1966, they have not always kept up with spending by this group. Moreover, Medicare has been subjected to a number of changes since 1981, some of which increased costs to beneficiaries. That is, benefit, premium, and cost-sharing changes directly affecting enrollees reduced Medicare benefits by about 5 percent over what would have been projected if there had been no legislation also affecting the share that beneficiaries pay (Moon 1993).[12] Altogether, Medicare and Medicaid cover about 63 percent of the costs of care for older persons. And of the remaining 37 percent, less than one-third of that is paid as part of the subsidies from retiree or employee insurance. Thus, it is true both that government subsidies are very large in dollar terms, but not as comprehensive as many believe.

CONCLUSION

How should we use this information to inform the debate over changes in entitlements for the elderly? Not all the elderly are rich; rather, the story is much more complicated. There is enormous diversity within the elderly population—a diversity likely to continue into the future as well. This means that there will likely be a clash between the goals of universal programs and the goals of more targeted ones in terms of shaping the future. The success of broad-based programs like Social Security and Medicare will be increasingly challenged by data suggesting that the needs of the populations served by these programs vary more than when they were established.

Although many statistics can be brought to bear to illustrate that spending on entitlements for the elderly is very high, not all of the needs of this age group of the population have been met. Poverty remains a problem for some elderly families, and the burdens of health care expenses are problematic for middle-income households as well as for those with more limited resources. Does this mean that no cuts can be made? It is unlikely that we will spare these programs in any effort to balance the budget, and there are certainly a number of areas where changes can and should be made, as is discussed in succeeding chapters. But these findings also suggest that care must be taken to protect those who are most vulnerable.

What about the share of federal dollars directed at the elderly overall? Viewpoints on the appropriate balance will be based on perceptions of how well off seniors are relative to younger families and individuals. The evidence concerning the well-being of elderly versus younger families is more difficult to sort out, since sources of well-being and needs of these groups vary substantially. This will make already-subjective decisions about cuts in programs directed at the elderly versus others more difficult.

One of the strengths of Social Security and Medicare is that whereas these programs have changed over time, we have still been able to retain the principles of social insurance. But this also illustrates that no one should assume an inviolable social contract prohibiting future adjustments in these programs. One of the greatest challenges for the future is that of keeping the promise of universal coverage while protecting programs like Medicaid that are designed to more carefully target benefits.

Notes

1. Growth rates in the top quintile of singles and the bottom quintile of couples were also low.

2. The Census Bureau has now modified its approach so that medical expenditures cannot remove from poverty anyone without enough income to pay income and housing expenses. But whereas this is an improvement, it essentially establishes a lower standard of poverty for those who receive any medical benefits from the government.

3. If these same numbers were calculated for the SIPP database, the percentages would be lower, but the relative differences would be very similar.

4. A new report on the measurement of poverty from the National Research Council (1995) basically concurs with many of the issues raised in the preceding paragraphs, and particularly with the impacts of health care needs.

5. Indeed, in another analysis not detailed here, we are calculating the annuity value that such assets confer. But this is more important for cross-age comparisons and for higher-income elderly persons in general.

6. The quintile rankings used here were set for all households, not just the elderly. Households in the bottom quintile have incomes of $12,852 per year or less. The cutoff for the top 20 percent is $53,448.

7. Recently released data from two other surveys on smaller subgroups of the population suggest that the SIPP data understate the level of assets likely for this group (Juster and Moon forthcoming).

8. These financial assets are, however, often a source of income for older persons that replace the earnings that younger families depend upon.

9. In 1990, when other income tax rates were raised, the rate on capital gains remained at 28 percent, restoring some of its preferential treatment—although to only a limited degree.

10. In addition to the traditional Medicaid protection for very low-income seniors, the Qualified Medicare Beneficiary (QMB) program was established in 1988 to specifically protect persons with below-poverty income from the deductibles, copayments, and premiums that Medicare requires. A recent study (Neumann et al. 1994) concluded that only about 41 percent of those eligible now participate.

11. Medicare has absorbed a considerable share of the costs of home health care, even though the latter was intended as a skilled benefit rather than a long-term care benefit.

12. The Medicaid long-term care program did not face as many cuts at the federal level, but fiscal pressures on states and strong demands for expanding care to younger Medicaid beneficiaries certainly have acted to slow any expansion in the long-term care portions of Medicaid. Moreover, in 1988 Medicaid was expanded with the addition of the Qualified Medicare Beneficiary program.

Chapter Three

UNDERSTANDING ENTITLEMENTS

In the constant search for ways to reduce the federal budget deficit, one of the newest slogans is to "cut entitlements"—or at least to slow their growth within the budget. Entitlement programs have been characterized as government giveaways that are out of control because people behave as though they are "entitled" to particular benefits. Indeed, many proponents of entitlement cuts incorrectly treat this as the official definition. But in actuality, *entitlement* is simply a budget term for programs that were intentionally established to be outside the usual appropriations process. They are a protected type of spending, in part to ensure predictability for those who qualify for benefits. Further, entitlements are sometimes mistakenly equated with "welfare" programs; in fact, some of those who decry spending on entitlements under this mistaken belief are likely to be supporters of the three programs that, as stated earlier, actually dominate that spending category—Social Security and Medicare.

In other cases, the justification for cutting entitlements simply focuses on their size as a share of the budget. Proponents of cuts also point to the long-run problems that will occur in financing these programs as baby boomers age. The 1995 Hospital Insurance (HI) trustees' *Annual Report*, which projects a depletion of the HI trust fund by 2002 (Board of Trustees, Federal HI Trust Fund 1995), has been adopted by the Republican Congress as a rationale for cutting Medicare in order to save the trust fund and, hence, to continue paying benefits (Seib 1995).

Interest in examining what should be done about entitlements is both a controversial issue and one that will likely be part of the political debate for some time to come. Controversial issues are sometimes avoided by politicians—for example, taking on Social Security has been likened to political suicide. Nonetheless, there seems at present to be a greater willingness to begin this discussion, at least in terms of the Medicare and Medicaid programs. The open question, however, is whether this debate will be straightforward or couched in various forms of rhetoric that prevent a more honest exchange.

DEFINING ENTITLEMENTS

The use of the term *entitlement* has undergone an interesting transformation. Until recently, the term was mainly used in budget circles to refer to programs that "make payments to any person, business, or unit of government that seeks the payments and that meets the eligibility established by law" (U.S. Congressional Budget Office [henceforth, CBO] 1992). Congress controls these programs indirectly by establishing rules for eligibility and benefits, rather than through the annual appropriation process. It is this budgetary characteristic that leads to a program being categorized as an entitlement. The U.S. Government Accounting Office offers a similar definition and adds: "Authorization for entitlements constitutes a binding obligation on the part of the Federal Government, and eligible recipients have legal recourse if the obligation is not fulfilled" (U.S. General Accounting Office [henceforth, GAO] 1981).

Entitlements comprise the bulk of "mandatory spending"—that is, all federal spending that occurs outside the appropriations process (Congressional Research Service [henceforth, CRS] 1994). Mandatory spending is the budget category usually reported by the Congressional Budget Office and the Office of Management and Budget in their various analyses. Entitlements account for 82 percent of mandatory spending (CBO 1994c); the remainder mostly comprises interest on the federal debt and payments for deposit insurance. These technical budget terms were originally established as ways to conveniently categorize the federal budget and not as groups of programs that necessarily share any common goal.

Mandatory spending replaced an older term used by budget experts, that of *relatively uncontrollable spending*. That term was thought to carry too negative a connotation. That is, these programs are not truly uncontrollable except in the context of being outside the normal process of authorizing new spending in each year's budget. Unless Congress amends these programs, outlays on mandatory spending depend only upon the application of the legislation that defines under what conditions spending occurs; in the case of entitlements, this means who is eligible and for what level of benefits. For example, if more people qualify for Social Security this year than last, and if their previous earnings are high, the annual rise in Social Security benefits will be large. These outlays on Social Security do not come up against a spending ceiling the way programs that require annual authorization do.[1] This is the sense in which they are termed *mandatory* or *uncontrollable*.

Nonetheless, at any time, Congress can change the operating rules of the program to achieve a different spending level. And indeed, these programs are often changed. For example, nearly every year since 1981, modifications in the Medicare program have been part of budget reconciliation legislation aimed at reducing federal spending (Moon 1993). If Congress does not act, however, the spending levels will still change "on their own."

Why are entitlements exempted from the annual appropriations process? It could well be argued that these programs were given special treatment to protect them from the annual debate on the budget. An entitlement program may thus be thought of as one established to be exempt from the vagaries of annual political wrangling, rather than carrying the negative connotation often associated with the term. For example, the Social Security program is allowed to bypass the annual appropriations process to assure people that they will receive the Social Security benefits promised in the legislation. As a result, the details of such programs are likely to change less frequently and thus provide stability and predictability for their beneficiaries. Retirement programs and income security programs need this stability and continuity over time if they are to serve as bases for protecting individuals in our society. Moreover, since Social Security was intended to be only part of retirement income for most Americans, people need predictability in order to plan their private retirement savings behavior. If benefit levels were raised or lowered each year, individuals would not be able to plan for their future retirement incomes.

In the case of the medical programs (Medicare and Medicaid), spending each year also needs to be flexible to respond to health care needs. The open-ended nature of health insurance in both the public and private sectors makes it difficult to establish before the fact what spending will or ought to be. Benefits are defined in terms of protection for necessary medical expenditures; differences in the costs of providing that coverage each year as a result of health care inflation result in increased spending. Moreover, technological change and new approaches to treatment mean that appropriate care will change over time. Thus, there are valid reasons for treating some programs outside the normal appropriations process.

Does this flexibility necessarily lead to more rapid spending growth? Although these programs are not subject to appropriations, there is nothing inherent in the category of entitlements itself that would necessarily lead to disproportionate growth in spending. That growth depends upon the eligibility and benefit definitions built into law. For example, very stringent rules might result in slow growth over time. As demonstrated later in this volume, each program differs in the actual growth that has occurred over time, reflecting special circumstances surrounding each. Indeed, programs like Social Security or unemployment compensation have sometimes been called "automatic stabilizers," and lauded for their higher growth in periods of low economic growth. They tend to replace income lost due to unemployment and recession.

Specific Programs Comprising the Entitlement Category

Many programs termed *entitlements* have little in common except their budgetary characteristics. They were enacted to serve quite different purposes. Some entitlements, for example, represent payments to other levels of government and to other countries to achieve various goals. Among the programs found in table 3.1 are farm price supports, education and training programs, traditional welfare programs, and unemployment compensation. Nonetheless, the largest entitlements are those that mainly benefit older Americans. As indicated earlier,

Table 3.1 CBO BASELINE PROJECTIONS OF MANDATORY OUTLAYS THROUGH 2000 (BY FISCAL YEAR, IN BILLIONS OF DOLLARS)

	Actual 1991	Actual 1994	1995	1996	2000	Change 1991–2000
Social Security	267	317	334	352	433	166
Medicare:	114	160	176	196	286	172
Part A	79	102	112	123	167	88
Part B	46	58	64	73	119	73
Medicaid	53	82	90	100	149	96
Civil Service, Military, and Railroad Retirement	64	72	75	77	96	32
Unemployment Compensation	25	26	22	23	28	3
Food Stamps	19	25	26	27	32	13
Supplemental Security Income	15	24	24	24	40	25
Family Support Payments	14	17	18	18	29	6
Veterans' Compensation and Pensions	16	21	20	20	24	8
Farm Price Supports	10	10	10	9	8	−2
Other Mandatory Spending	39	34	50	52	53	14
Total Mandatory Outlays	636	788	845	898	1169	533

Source: U.S. Congressional Budget Office 1995c.
Note: Projections are from the Congressional Budget Office (CBO) baseline in January 1995. Some baseline numbers may have changed slightly since then.

Social Security is the largest entitlement program, followed by Medicare. Medicaid, with a large share going to the elderly, and other federal retirement programs also comprise an important share of the total.[2] Altogether, Medicare, Medicaid, and Social Security account for 68.5 percent of all entitlements (CBO 1994c).

Almost by definition, to consider changes in entitlements as a way of reducing federal spending is to implicitly take on programs for older Americans who are the major beneficiaries across the range of entitlement spending. But not all the spending on programs associated with older Americans is confined to that group. Just 78 percent of Social Security payments go to the elderly, for example, and 89 percent of Medicare benefits. An overall analysis of the major entitlement programs that benefit the elderly indicated that in 1990, the share that went to persons aged 65 and older was about 71 percent (U.S. House 1993). If all entitlement programs could be allocated by age group, about two-thirds of the benefits would be dedicated to seniors.[3]

Inherent in the recognition of the size of Social Security and Medicare is the fact that entitlements do not primarily refer to welfare programs.[4] The misunderstanding that *entitlement* is synonymous with *welfare* has also contributed to a pejorative characterization of entitlements as connoting benefits to "undeserving" recipients. In fact, after an article about entitlements ran in the *News Bulletin* of the American Association of Retired Persons, many older persons wrote to the association indicating outrage that Social Security was treated as a welfare program by classifying it and Medicare as "entitlements" (Carlson 1994). Means-tested programs constitute just over one in every five entitlement dollars (CBO 1994c), and if Medicaid were excluded, that proportion would shrink to 12 percent. Thus, if there is an entitlement problem, it is associated with Social Security and the two health care programs, and not with welfare.

Spending Growth and Entitlements

There is another way in which any discussion of entitlements is inexorably intertwined with Social Security, Medicare, and Medicaid spending on the elderly. The view of entitlements as a category of spending that is out of control is only appropriate for the programs associated with seniors, and in particular the two health care entitlements. From 1975 to 1993, spending on all entitlements increased by an annual average rate of 8.9 percent, compared to a 6.9 percent rate of growth in defense and a 7.1 percent growth rate for domestic discretionary spending (see figure 3.1). But if Medicare, Medicaid, and

Figure 3.1 AVERAGE ANNUAL RATES OF GROWTH OF FEDERAL SPENDING,
1975–93

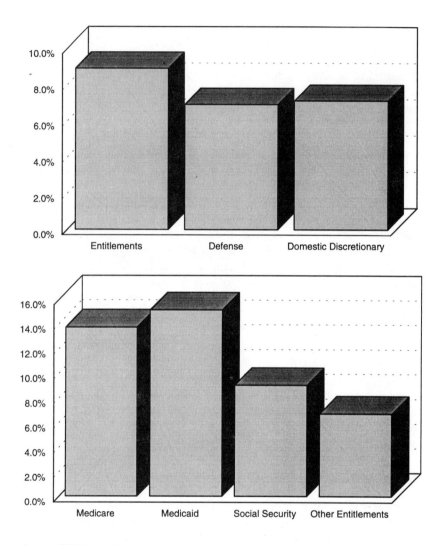

Source: CBO (1994c).

Social Security are singled out, the annual rate of growth was 10.6 percent, while that for all other entitlements grew by only 6.3 percent—less than that for other discretionary spending (figure 3.1) (CBO 1994c).

Entitlement programs have traditionally enjoyed the highest public support among all government programs, so their growth is not particularly a surprise. The slow growth of means-tested programs (other than Medicaid) would likely disarm some of the critics of entitlements. Again, it is probably deceptive to criticize "entitlements" per se.[5]

Another way in which the growth of entitlements has been highlighted is to project their future share of the federal budget. This is a useful exercise, but only if one understands the rules of budget accounting. These programs are formally projected to grow on the basis of eligibility and benefit projections—an appropriate set of criteria. But all programs that are subject to the appropriations process are merely frozen at current spending levels. This assumes no policy choices and results in the self-fulfilling prophecy that entitlements will grow faster than other programs. Thus, any projection of future budget "baselines" can be somewhat misleading. It is only true that entitlements will necessarily edge out all other spending if we make no changes in policy—an unlikely prospect. Such a claim is thus essentially a consequence of the conventions used in making future projections and the aging of the population and rising health care costs.

On the other hand, since entitlement programs are intended to change only slowly over time, cost projections are particularly important. If the programs are growing so rapidly as to threaten their survival, early warning is essential. Indeed, both Social Security and the Hospital Insurance portion of Medicare have trust funds that help to track the balance between financing and program outlays. The annual report on these trust funds seeks to provide such early warning (this is discussed in the next section).

Thus, it is important to recognize that the congressional intent of such programs was that they would grow unencumbered by politics (although it is also likely that few lawmakers expected such rapid growth). It is appropriate to periodically reevaluate whether such preferential treatment is still desired and whether the same level of commitment is appropriate. But if this special budget treatment is deemed to be warranted, the growth of entitlements should be viewed as an *intended* consequence over time. If not, then like other government programs, the entitlements in question need to be amended.

Finally, some of those who debate this issue are questioning the virtue of ever establishing entitlement programs. Should all spending at the federal level require a yearly review? Should all programs have to compete against each other on an equal footing? This is a broader, budgetary issue that is largely beyond the scope of this volume, but lurks in the background of this debate. The discussion is complicated by the mistaken belief that entitlements by their nature expand rapidly and thus are out of control. If this were a problem inherent to entitlements, then annual reviews might be justified, but as discussed earlier, it is not entitlement per se but the specific program that matters.

THE SOCIAL INSURANCE TRUST FUNDS

Since Social Security and part of Medicare are financed by a dedicated payroll (Federal Insurance Contribution Act [FICA]) tax, the revenues and outflows are tracked by means of trust funds. These trust funds allow an analysis of how well the financing mechanisms are succeeding in paying for the benefits covered by these programs. The Social Security program has two separate trust funds, one for disability insurance (DI) and the other for old-age, survivors, and dependents benefits (OASI). Medicare also has two trust funds, for Hospital Insurance (HI) and Supplementary Medical Insurance (SMI). In the case of Medicare, however, much less attention is directed at the SMI trust fund, since it is kept in balance by general revenues.

As stated earlier, by law, an annual report is issued on the financial outlook of each of these trust funds over an extended period. Of necessity, many assumptions need to be made to project what spending and revenue will look like 30 or 40 years into the future. In 1995, for example, the trust fund reports indicate that under an intermediate set of assumptions, the OASI trust fund will be exhausted in the year 2030 (Board of Trustees, Federal OASDI Trust Funds 1995). That is of concern, but far enough into the future that no immediate crisis is perceived. In fact, the current balance in the OASI trust fund is over 400 billion dollars and is projected to continue rising for some time to come.

On the other hand, Medicare's HI trust fund is in a much more precarious position, with exhaustion of the trust fund balance projected for the year 2002 (Board of Trustees, Federal HI Trust Fund 1995). Without a change in policy, the balance in the trust fund will drop rapidly from now until 2002, and the trustees' report warns that action needs to be taken immediately to begin to alleviate this problem.

Medicare has faced this problem before. For example, the 1993 trust fund report suggested that the funds would be exhausted by 1999. And as early as 1970, there were reports predicting exhaustion of the funds within 7 years (O'Sullivan 1995). In each case, policy changes have been enacted that pushed back the projections. But in 1995 there has been much greater attention to this looming crisis. Part of the explanation for this is purely political. Republicans discovered in the HI trust fund report (Board of Trustees, Federal HI Trust Fund 1995)— often treated in the past as a relatively obscure document—a rationale for the substantial changes they proposed for the 1996 budget and beyond. This has offered the Republicans political cover from Demo-. cratic attacks on these Medicare cuts (Seib 1995).

Thus, while some of the rhetoric concerning what will happen to Medicare in 2002 is overblown, the problem is more severe now than in earlier years because we are closer to imbalance than at many times in the past. That is, we are beginning to draw down the trust fund, whereas earlier projections usually still had several years before that began. Once that process begins, the order of magnitude of the problem accelerates. When the trust fund balance declines, interest payments, which currently run in excess of $10 billion a year, also fall, speeding the rate of decline. And the dollars needed to solve the problem are higher than ever before. This is also a difficult period, since the antitax sentiment among politicians makes it difficult to consider a wider range of options than simply cutting benefits to solve this problem.

COMMON ISSUES FOR ANY ASSESSMENT OF ENTITLEMENTS

Of necessity, entitlements will be closely scrutinized for the foreseeable future. Even if substantial cuts in Medicare and Medicaid are enacted in 1995, pressure to consider further changes will continue. The political environment may change, making entitlements more or less vulnerable, but this debate will not be put to rest until after most of the baby boom generation has retired. The aging of the population and health-cost-driven growth in Medicare and Medicaid result in projections in which entitlements for the elderly will consume an ever-larger share of the federal budget over time.

As suggested in the early part of this chapter, Americans need to carefully assess the appropriate role of entitlements in our society. However, the current rhetoric tends to be alarmist, often ignoring issues that would balance the debate. The themes discussed in the following paragraphs should be part of any assessment of the future of entitlements.

Short- versus Long-run Savings

Reductions in Social Security and Medicare carry the implicit promise of killing two birds with one stone—reducing the current budget deficit of the federal government and helping the long-run stability of the trust funds that finance these two programs. The problem is that these two time frames do not mesh very well. Savings that help the federal deficit over the next few years may not be the best long-run strategies for the trust funds. Social Security and Medicare play a unique role in the lives of Americans in that they promise a floor of income protection during retirement. Many Americans conscientiously make savings and other decisions on the basis of what they expect to receive from Social Security. Moreover, once individuals retire, it is difficult to return to the labor force or to make other changes to compensate for benefit reductions that would apply to existing beneficiaries. It is thus important for these programs to change slowly over time to remain valuable sources of protection for retirees. These factors make short-run savings efforts less desirable unless they are part of a longer-term strategy.

But there may be a different rationale for making some short-run changes in these programs. The demographic challenges of the future that dictate important changes in Social Security and Medicare will require reductions in financial support for many future retirees. If we begin to put these changes into law so that future plans can be made, it may be reasonable to seek some short-run sacrifices from current beneficiaries as well, in a spirit of shared sacrifice. And since such short-run changes should help the federal deficit, that will be a contribution to future generations. But deciding what the appropriate balance should be constitutes a difficult task.

Redistribution as Important Component of Social Insurance

One of the easiest things to forget in evaluating entitlement programs is that they were established explicitly to redistribute resources. A principal characteristic of social insurance is its requirement that people contribute on the basis of ability to pay, while receiving benefits according to criteria that include need. That is, Social Security and Medicare are not just bank accounts where the issue is whether you get a "fair return" on your investment. Social insurance is more complicated and needs to be assessed in terms of all its goals. "Money's worth" types of calculations that focus on return of "investment" in the program are interesting but offer a limited picture of the success of these programs. It is certainly inappropriate to treat them as the sole measure of success.

The traditional notion of social insurance in Social Security, for example, is that it is redistributive within a particular age cohort, paying more as a share of earlier income to those with few resources, and less to those with more resources. Finding differential rates of return under Social Security between the rich and poor is thus a goal and not just a random phenomenon that people have observed. Similarly, while it is instructive to consider differences in rates of return over time, some redistribution across age cohorts is also consistent with the principles of social insurance. Higher relative Social Security and Medicare payments went to earlier generations whose incomes were substantially lower than today's retirees. Criticism that centers on declining rates of return over time may thus also be misleading. Distributional comparisons are only telling if we have a normative sense of our goals. Indeed, declining rates of return may be considered a measure of success in aiding earlier cohorts, and enforce realism that such returns are not affordable in the future.

Including Offsetting Expansions with Any Big Changes

One of the dangers of public policy is that we have a history of promising broad-based special protections for those most disadvantaged by major policy shifts. The problem is that these special protections seldom materialize. After a period of time, we find that the public's memory is short, and safeguards that would require additional resources are forgotten and never enacted. Hence, supporters of programs have a right to be skeptical about promises for later relief should problems arise.

One of the best examples of how promises of offsetting expansions to accompany major cuts never materialize is the deinstitutionalization of a substantial share of America's mentally ill population in the 1970s and 80s. The policy seemed sound: move people out of large mental hospitals where people were "warehoused" and into smaller, community-based settings where they would have greater opportunities to return to the mainstream. The deinstitutionalization proceeded rapidly, but the development of residential care facilities did not keep pace. As a consequence, many of the mentally ill have slipped out of the system. They receive little or no care and are likely to be homeless and destitute. Our enthusiasm for cutting back expenditures in one area was simply greater than the commitment to finding stable environments elsewhere for these people. The direct costs of government have declined, but the quality of life for many mentally ill individuals who fell through the cracks has also declined.

Another example can be found in the Medicare program. The inpatient hospital payment system was changed substantially beginning in 1984. These reforms were intended to make hospital care more efficient, and an expected side effect was the earlier discharge of patients from hospitals. Arguments in favor of this change emphasized that patients would be better served in less-intensive settings— for example, in skilled nursing facilities (SNFs) or at home with supportive medical services. But at the same time that the hospital payment changes went into effect, leading to rapid declines in hospital lengths of stay, relief for those who still needed care was not forthcoming (Moon 1993). The Medicare SNF and home health benefits were being tightly controlled and discouraged from expanding. As a consequence, the savings to government were greater than they otherwise would have been, but at the expense of some Medicare patients. Studies of the hospital payment system have suggested that some patients were discharged too soon in unstable condition (Kahn et al. 1990). In this case, the hospital payment system is not necessarily bad, but the coordination to ensure an adequate safety net for postacute care did not occur. It may be just too tempting to forgo the added expense of more protections if the public outcry is not large enough.

Thus, if entitlements move in the direction of reducing benefits or eligibility on the grounds that less-extensive coverage is warranted, it is important to ensure that any exceptions to protect certain groups are enacted concurrent with any cuts. This issue may become more critical in the near future, since some of the debate over how to reduce spending over time on Medicare and Medicaid has focused on limiting the rate at which programs will be allowed to grow over time. The appeal of such an approach is that it sounds quite technical, but does not identify who might be affected. Moreover, proponents argue that these are not "cuts" but only restrictions in the growth of the programs. Caps do not solve the problem of what or how to cut; they simply mandate that some change occurs. Further, to the extent that cuts are enacted with few protections for beneficiaries, it may be difficult to later undo any problems that arise. This caution assumes even more importance if, for example, caps on the rate of growth of Medicaid are coupled with increased flexibility to states. Some of the protections now found in Medicaid for various groups may well erode over time in the name of "flexibility."

How Effective Can We Be at Better Targeting?

One focus of the options considered in this volume is to achieve a better targeted benefit in a number of areas, perhaps even shifting resources from one program to another. But many important practical problems need to be resolved to target entitlements to some groups more than others.

First, some expense would be necessary to achieve further targeting. For example, the Medicare program now makes benefits equally available to everyone. Altering that would require new administrative structures and the necessity to test the incomes or assets of beneficiaries. Such efforts are not only expensive but unpopular. Achieving accuracy in any targeting is also likely to be expensive.

Since no system of targeting is apt to be error free, a major philosophical question is whether a chosen monitoring system places more emphasis on ensuring that policies we adopt err in the direction of underpaying or of overpaying beneficiaries. That is, it is difficult to design a system that does not treat some people unfairly. And if errors are to be made, would we prefer relatively laxer standards that will be overly generous in some cases, or more stringent standards that will sometimes result in undue hardships? For example, if there is to be some means testing of benefits, will we use only an income test or also screen individuals for their asset holdings as well? Stringent standards are likely to be more expensive to administer, which might weigh as another factor in choosing how we try to target benefits.

Welfare programs, with attention to reducing fraud and limiting dependency over time, use restrictive and sometimes punitive approaches to targeting. This philosophy seems to run counter to the goals of more targeting within universal coverage. If the emphasis is instead on marginal shifts to ensure that the vulnerable are well protected while limiting any new commitments to the programs, then the standards for targeting could be considerably less stringent than those found in traditional welfare programs.[6]

But laxity in targeting can lead to "gaming" of the system—where people hide income or assets in order to qualify. This has, for example, been a continuing problem in the Medicaid program's eligibility determinations for receipt of long-term care services. And when there is even a perception of such gaming, support for a program is likely to be undermined.

Whatever the philosophical approach, a number of dilemmas will arise in putting more targeting into practice. Should we add whole new mechanisms to check income status for receipt of Medicare, for example, or should we rely on the Internal Revenue Service (IRS) as the means for targeting? Moreover, as discussed in chapter 2, there is considerable disagreement in the policy community about how best to measure differences in economic status. Since older persons rely on assets and asset income for a substantial share of their well-being, does this mean it is essential to test assets as well as income? Also, how do we ensure that equals are treated equally—for example, through adjustments for family size?

Choosing a Socially Acceptable Level for Further Targeting

Despite the temptation to treat entitlement programs as unnecessary for the protection of elderly persons, the facts (see chapter 2) suggest that dramatic changes in Social Security, Medicare, and Medicaid could have profound impacts on those over age 65. Much of the well-being of moderate-income older Americans depends upon these programs.

Consequently, perhaps the most difficult issue for achieving improved targeting is to determine at what point benefits or eligibility should begin to change. Who should be included in "protected" categories when benefits are reduced or eliminated for others? This is a highly charged, normative question likely to influence both what resources could be freed up for other purposes and the popularity of the modified programs. Adopting stringent limits for eligibility would reduce substantially the level of spending by converting these programs essentially into welfare benefits. But we already have in place Medicaid and Supplemental Security Income, corresponding welfare programs that have as yet failed to fully cover the poor among the elderly. To differentiate Social Security and Medicare, some have proposed limiting eligibility to middle- and lower-income households. Eligibility for upper-income families and individuals would be phased out. But how should we define *middle income*?

A central premise of this chapter has been that entitlements should be judged on their own merits and not as areas ripe for budget cutting merely because that is where the spending is concentrated. This also means putting issues of fairness in the context of sacrifices being proposed elsewhere in the federal budget and tax structure. For example, do we hold to the same standards of protecting "middle-income" families across all federal programs? In dealing with questions of fairness, two principles are often applied: horizontal and vertical equity. The first, horizontal equity, is the goal of treating individuals who are alike equally. This is often applied to evaluate whether we are treating families of different size fairly. But it can also be used to ask whether we use the same standards across programs in treating people fairly. Vertical equity refers to varying treatment by people's economic status, usually implying more generous treatment (or lower taxes) for those with fewer resources. Again, this might be applied across both tax and spending programs. Thus, there is considerable room for debate on appropriate targeting, but it should not be confined to one program or even one category of public programs.

CONCLUSIONS

The task of developing reasonable options for changes in entitlements is a formidable one. The political machinations that occurred in the 1994 congressional elections and the beginnings of the 1995 budget debate offer just the most recent examples of how sweeping promises can preclude a true debate on the issues. Both those who argue for no change under any conditions and those who would dramatically cut successful programs do a disservice to the goal of finding workable solutions to the future challenges that entitlements will surely face.

The chapters following endeavor to sort out some of the key issues that need investigating. None of the choices are easy ones, but some options hold more promise than others.

Notes

1. The exception is the Food Stamp program, which is subject to the appropriations process and has a mechanism for reducing benefits if necessary once the ceiling has been reached. This program has sometimes been referred to as a "capped entitlement."

2. For example, in 1992, about 30 percent of Medicaid went to persons aged 65 and older (Coughlin, Holahan, and Ku 1994).

Chapter Four

SOCIAL SECURITY

When discussions about "protecting promises" arise in the entitlement debate in Congress, Social Security represents the most sacred promise of all. During the 1994 congressional elections, both Democrats and Republicans recognized the importance of reducing entitlements, but, at the same time, they promised that the largest entitlement program, Social Security, would be protected. The reluctance of legislators to alter Social Security reflects its universal appeal, in general, but also the political power of the elderly. The reality is, however, that Social Security faces financial problems that need to be addressed sooner rather than later.

Recent projections by Social Security actuaries indicate that the trust fund will be exhausted by the year 2030 as the last of the baby boomers enter retirement (Board of Trustees, Federal OASDI Trust Funds 1995). Although this date seems far in the future, the long-term solvency issue needs to be considered soon for a number of reasons. First, the earlier the issue is addressed, the less draconian the changes will have to be. Second, to the extent that future beneficiaries are notified of potential changes, they will be better able to adjust their planning and behavior now. And, third, for at least a perception of fairness, it may be important to begin to modify benefits for current Social Security recipients as part of a gradual set of changes.

Solutions to these long-run problems are not easy. Either revenues must be raised or spending cut. Considering the strong sentiment by both political parties to avoid tax increases, the possibility of raising revenues is very unlikely, at least in the near future. This places the emphasis on reducing Social Security benefits over time.

While we might find agreement that benefits need to be cut over time, some short-run questions arise in this context as well: Whose benefits should be reduced and by how much? and When should we begin to make such changes? Some would say current beneficiaries should be affected because their benefits are already too generous. Others would contend, however, that current benefits are insufficient to meet the daily needs of the 4 million poor elderly. What about the fact that future beneficiaries are expected to live longer and thus gain more years of benefits than earlier retirees? At the same time, compared to current beneficiaries, future Social Security recipients will have contributed far more into the system during their working years. All of these various factors can be cited to make a case on either side of the issue of whether current beneficiaries need to face cuts in benefits.

Adding to the impetus to consider changes now in Social Security is the opportunity to improve the Social Security system, correct some inequities, and better target benefits. Although Social Security is expected to be fiscally sound for many years to come, the Medicare Hospital Insurance (HI) and the Disability Insurance (DI) trust funds are expected to be exhausted by the years 2002 and 2016, respectively. Since these programs are closely related to Social Security they should not be ignored. Problems in these trust funds will inevitably affect the Old-Age and Survivors Insurance (OASI) portion, and attempts to siphon off OASI funds for shortfalls may comprise some of the options suggested to protect HI and DI. Finally, as argued earlier regarding entitlements, it makes little sense to consider Social Security in isolation from other crucial public programs for older Americans. It may be possible to explicitly or implicitly aid Medicare and even Medicaid with some changes in Social Security. Specifics of such trade-offs are considered in chapter 7.

HOW SHOULD WE BEGIN?

Any serious debate over how soon Social Security benefits should begin to be scaled back and by how much depends on an assessment of the adequacy of current and future Social Security benefits. To assess what might be desirable in terms of new directions, it is relevant to ask to what extent the program has achieved its goals. To do this we consider several key questions.

- Does Social Security meet the goals outlined in the original legislation and later modifications?
- Does Social Security meet the needs of its beneficiaries (on the whole and in terms of various subgroups)?
- Has Social Security struck a reasonable balance between the workers who contribute and those who currently benefit from the pro-

gram? How does this affect perceptions about intergenerational fairness?

- Have we overpromised benefits for the future relative to our ability to pay for them?

Historical Context

One way to pose arguments concerning the present and future of Social Security is to examine the program's legislative history. What was the intent of the program? What were its original goals and limits? Such an examination can provide justifications for the positions of both critics and supporters of Social Security. As with any piece of major social legislation, Social Security's passage mixed the motives and goals of many different lawmakers. Some viewed the legislation as activity that would help to mitigate economic downturns like that experienced in the 1930s. In fact, early in the process, much of the attention of the Committee on Economic Security—a cabinet-level group assigned by President Franklin Roosevelt to develop legislation—focused on unemployment compensation rather than retirement (Achenbaum 1986). Other supporters of public pensions proclaimed Social Security as the beginning of a new approach to old age in America that would forever change our treatment of retirees. In contrast, some critics of Social Security look back on its genesis as a unique period in history that we have outgrown, and with it our need for the Social Security program as we know it (Peterson and Howe 1988).

One aspect of Social Security made clear at passage of the original legislation in 1935 was that the program was to combine assistance and insurance—a characteristic that remains today. That is, Social Security was designed to establish a floor of security to protect those with the lowest lifetime earnings, and above that to allow the benefits to rise for workers who made greater contributions. The formula that was generated essentially returns higher payments as a share of contributions to persons with the lowest average earnings, while still paying more to those who contributed more into the system. The formula has been altered over time, but the basic premise of its "progressive" structure has not changed.[1] This characteristic of the program makes simple judgments about fairness and adequacy more difficult, however, since by design, benefits are not the same for all participants.

In addition, Social Security was not intended to be a full wage replacement program. The assumption has always been that other forms of retirement income would be necessary to maintain a reasonable standard of living. Moreover, those with higher incomes were expected to supplement an even greater share of their incomes from other sources. Consequently, the formula used to determine benefits replaces only a portion of earlier wages, and as wages rise, the formula becomes less generous.

Both of these concepts are captured in the "replacement rate"—one measure used to illustrate the generosity of Social Security benefits. This figure is a percentage indicating how retirement benefits (taken at the normal retirement age) compare to pre-retirement earnings. Although it is generally agreed that benefits should amount to a portion of pre-retirement earnings, the exact share is subject to debate. It should also be noted that the replacement rate is higher for low-wage workers and lower for high-wage earners—reflecting the deliberate use of a formula that is more generous to those who have lower earnings over their lifetimes, demonstrating the program's progressivity.

As shown in table 4.1, an average worker retiring in 1940 could have expected only a 26 percent replacement rate (U.S. House, 1994). After the early expansions in the Social Security program, in which the rate grew in an ad hoc fashion, the 1972 amendments sought to stabilize the rate by adjusting for inflation. But because of an error in the formula adopted in 1972, the replacement rate grew at an unprecedented clip for persons born between 1911 and 1916. This error was corrected in the 1977 amendments.[2] The replacement ratio for average ₊workers now hovers just over 40 percent. Thus, Social Security's generosity has risen over time, but the share that a person born in 1975 can expect is quite similar to what someone born in 1910 would have received. Rates of high- and low-wage workers have also changed in a similar pattern over time, except that there is a continued slow rise for high-wage workers into the future. With the exception of the early years of the program, the level of generosity has not changed much over time as measured by the replacement ratio.

Another way to look at this issue, however, focuses more on a lifetime perspective that factors in the length of time that beneficiaries draw benefits from the system compared to the number of years they contribute to it in the form of taxes. This accounts for changes in life expectancy over time and, hence, the number of years that someone would draw on Social Security benefits. For example, Steuerle and Bakija (1994) found that a two-earner couple earning average wages had a benefit-to-tax ratio of 7.67 if they retired in 1960. By 1990, that

Table 4.1 SOCIAL SECURITY REPLACEMENT RATES, 1940–2040

Year of Birth	Year of Attaining Normal Retirement Age	Replacement Rates (%)		
		Low Earner[a]	Average Earner[b]	Maximum Earner[c]
1875	1940	39.4	26.2	16.5
1885	1950	33.2	19.7	21.2
1895	1960	49.1	33.3	29.8
1900	1965	45.6	31.4	32.9
1905	1970	48.5	34.3	29.2
1910	1975	59.9	42.3	30.1
1911	1976	60.1	43.7	32.1
1912	1977	61.0	44.8	33.5
1913	1978	63.4	46.7	34.7
1914	1979	64.4	48.1	36.1
1915	1980	68.1	51.1	32.5
1916	1981	72.5	54.4	33.4
1917	1982	65.8	48.7	28.6
1918	1983	63.5	45.8	26.3
1919	1984	62.6	42.8	23.7
1920	1985	61.1	40.9	22.8
1921	1986	60.3	41.1	23.1
1922	1987	59.5	41.2	22.6
1923	1988	58.4	40.9	23.0
1924	1989	57.9	41.6	24.1
1925	1990	58.2	43.2	24.5
1935	1991	57.1	42.4	25.6
1944	2010	56.0	41.7	27.1
1954	2020	56.0	41.7	27.8
1963	2030	55.7	41.5	27.6
1973	2040	55.7	41.5	27.5

a. Earnings equal to 45 percent of "SSA average index."
b. Earnings equal to "SSA average wage index."
c. Earnings equal to the maximum wage taxable for Social Security purposes.

ratio had declined to 5.16, and by 1995 it had declined again to 3.83. Current beneficiaries are paying far more in taxes than their parents relative to what they will withdraw even though they will draw benefits for a greater number of years. And although these numbers will continue declining, much of the drop has already occurred. The same hypothetical couple retiring in 2010 would have a benefit-to-tax ratio of only 1.18.

Another early characteristic of Social Security that may affect an analysis of adequacy was the limited nature of the initial benefits established in 1935. The original legislation covered only workers. Moreover, the legislation precluded any payments under the retirement system until 1942 at the earliest. But Social Security remained on the political agenda, with numerous calls for expansions of various sorts and some concern about the drag on the economy that would come from building a large reserve (while tax contributions were made but no benefits were paid out). Consequently, the program was expanded in the 1939 amendments (Achenbaum 1986), extending coverage to dependents and survivors, and accelerating the payout of benefits. No longer was Social Security limited to workers, and no longer were benefits to be tied so closely to contributions. This marked a major liberalization of the program.

Major expansions in Social Security occurred again in 1950, and continued intermittently into the 1970s with ad hoc increases in benefits and coverage. These benefit increases more than compensated workers for inflation, which otherwise would have cut the value of benefits over time (Schulz et al. 1974). These changes reflect a society sharing its economic growth with its retired citizens. Moreover, the impact of this generosity can be seen in the sharp declines in poverty among the elderly that occurred in the 1960s and 1970s (as shown in chapter 2). Legislation continued to indicate support for generous benefits to an ever-broader portion of the population, achieving nearly universal coverage of workers by 1965 (Ball 1978). Most of this legislation passed with little objection or criticism.

What, then, can be concluded about the intended generosity or stability of the program? If we focus only on the original legislation, then Social Security as we know it today is more expansive than intended. But if we look at the pattern of amendments over time— which speaks to the intent of several generations of legislators—there is a long history of sharing economic growth with retirees. That is, as the economic well-being of workers increased in the 1950s and 1960s, benefits for retirees were increased substantially. In that way, retirees were able to benefit from economic growth.

Overall, the generosity of the program as now projected for the future is not out of line with where it has been for over 20 years. But the ad hoc adjustments of the past, which implicitly recognized the changing circumstances of younger workers, could be used as a justification to make changes now in a downward direction. Slower wage growth and shorter working lives, as well as demographic shifts, may be viewed as cautionary signals for a less-generous Social Security program in the future.

Social Security and Needs of Beneficiaries

Alternatively, rather than looking at the historical record, the question of adequacy of benefits could focus only on whether Social Security is meeting the needs of America's elderly citizens. This raises issues concerning both program characteristics for current beneficiaries as well as how fast we should alter the program over time.

One measure of adequacy is the poverty rate among the elderly, discussed in chapter 2. Since the inception of Social Security, the overall poverty rate has declined considerably. In 1966, more than 28 percent of the elderly were categorized as poor, as compared to only 12.2 percent nearly 30 years later. Much of this decline in poverty followed Social Security expansions in 1954 and 1972 (Schulz et al. 1974); that is, Social Security can be credited for much of this improvement.

Some advocates of scaling back Social Security point to these improvements as evidence that the economic status of the elderly has improved so much that they could bear substantial cuts in benefits. Such a rationale fails to look beyond the averages, however. Overall improvements in poverty rates mask much of the diversity among the elderly. The 4 million elderly who were poor in 1992 were largely concentrated among those over age 85, women, minorities, and persons living alone (Census Bureau 1993b). Nearly 15.7 percent of elderly women were impoverished in 1992, compared to only 8.7 percent of elderly men. The situation worsens for minorities. Nearly 26.8 percent of elderly black men and 37.7 percent of elderly black women were poor in 1992. The incidence of poverty also increases with age. Individuals over age 85 had poverty rates of 19.7 percent in 1992, and women aged 85 and over had poverty rates of 22.7 percent.

Many of these discrepancies in economic well-being mirror the fact that because Social Security benefits reflect wages of various groups earlier in life, minorities and never-married women do not fare as well as white males. Widows face lower incomes due to rules for survivors that generally result in a sharp drop in benefits and high poverty rates among women living alone—i.e., 22.8 percent as compared to 6.4 percent for married women (Census Bureau 1993b). Many of these individuals rely heavily on Social Security to provide the barest of necessities. Consequently, across-the-board cuts could adversely affect them.

Thus, although Social Security has been successful in reducing poverty rates among the elderly, this success does not itself justify future cuts. Rather, some might argue that there is still much to be done to enhance the economic well-being of the 4 million elderly who remain impoverished, perhaps by redirecting resources through improvements in the targeting of benefits.[3]

Intergenerational Comparisons

Another benchmark for judgments about Social Security is whether benefits are reasonable in comparison to the standard of living of younger families who are currently paying taxes to support these benefit levels. Since Social Security operates largely on a pay-as-you-go basis, it is natural to inquire whether those who fund the program are as well off as the recipients of these payments, particularly considering that incomes for many Americans did not grow rapidly, if at all, in the 1970s, 1980s, and early 1990s. Is the expansion of Social Security legislation of the 1950s, 1960s, and early 1970s (reflecting earlier economic growth) putting the economic status of retirees ahead of that of workers? An affirmative response could justify a downward shift in benefits. Moreover, the distribution of workers' earnings between high- and low-wage earners might be an issue as well.

There are a number of alternative ways to measure these intergenerational comparisons. The most straightforward way is to compare incomes of the young and old. For example, in 1992, the median income of households headed by persons under age 65 was $35,639. For households headed by persons aged 65 or older the median income stood at $17,160. This may be somewhat misleading, however, since younger households are larger than older ones.[4] If we examine, instead, per capita incomes, the figures would be closer—for example, $22,013 for men under age 65 and $14,548 for men aged 65 and older (Census Bureau 1993a). And if after-tax incomes were examined, the amounts would be closer still.

Between 1962 and 1984, the elderly's income growth outstripped increases in income for the population under age 65. For example, Radner (1993) found that the ratio of aged to nonaged median incomes (adjusted for size of family unit) rose from .526 to .727 over that period (see table 4.2). Although average before-tax incomes for elderly families still lagged behind those of younger families, after adjusting for differences in family size and tax liabilities, the disposable (post-tax) incomes of older Americans began to compare favorably with those of the young. In fact, some researchers have claimed that the overall well-being of the elderly now is on a par with or even exceeds that of younger families (Danziger et al. 1984; Smeeding 1986).

Table 4.2 RATIO OF AGED TO NONAGED FAMILY UNIT MEDIAN INCOMES,
ADJUSTED FOR SIZE OF UNIT AND AGE, SELECTED YEARS, 1967–90

Year	Ratio	Year	Ratio
1967	0.526	1984	0.727
1972	0.572	1985	0.712
1977	0.603	1986	0.706
1979	0.604	1987	0.687
1980	0.631	1988	0.693
1981	0.668	1989	0.693
1982	0.699	1990	0.725
1983	0.710		

Sources: Radner (1993).

A closer look at the timing of these changes is also instructive.
Between 1984 and 1989, the economic status of elderly families declined relative to that of the young, with the ratio of aged to nonaged
adjusted income falling to .693 (table 4.2). It then bounced up again
to .725 during the recession year of 1990. Inevitably, in some years
one group will gain relative to the other. For instance, the early 1980s
were a period of decelerating inflation, and lags in Social Security
payments are likely to have helped the elderly "catch up" relative to
the young. Further, older Americans are less sensitive to upturns in
unemployment, so as expected, that ratio rose again in 1990 and
would likely be high in 1991 and 1992 when the U.S. was experiencing
a recession. Changes in median income over the period suggest that
indeed this is what happened. Median income for households with
heads aged 65 and older grew by 8.8 percent (in nominal dollars)
between 1989 and 1992, but by only 7.9 percent for those under age
65 (Census Bureau 1993a).

Another way to focus on this issue examines the current baby boomers
compared to their parents. The baby boom generation (i.e. those individuals born between 1946 and 1964) will soon swell the ranks of retirees. Although recent evidence suggests that baby boomers may be financially better off than their parents' generation (CBO 1993), this
improvement in economic well-being is skewed toward individuals who
are better educated and married. Generally, baby boomers have median
household incomes 35 percent higher than their parents. But individuals
without a high school education and unmarried individuals with children have lower median incomes than their parents (CBO 1993). Homeownership also plays an important role in the economic well-being of
the baby boomers. Nonhomeowners may be unable to accumulate suffi-

cient wealth to afford a comfortable life style. In fact, lesser-educated and lower-income baby boomers are expected to fare more poorly than today's retirees in similar circumstances. This implies that under the current Social Security benefit structure, poverty rates among women and minorities aged 65 and over in the next century may even be higher than today. As a result, the progressivity of Social Security benefits is likely to continue to be a critical issue.

In addition to income comparisons, the potential well-being of the baby boomers and the generation that follows them in retirement hinges on their accumulation of wealth. Although wealth/income ratios are higher for boomers than for their parents 30 years earlier, that accumulation is also uneven. For example, singles and individuals aged 25 to 34 in the lower-income quintile are worse off than their parents. More important, much of the wealth accumulation for people aged 25 to 44 (for all but the top quintiles) is enough to support only one or two years of consumption (Sabelhaus and Manchester 1994). It is no wonder that many analysts concerned about future retirees focus on increasing the national savings rate.

Future Prospects

Even though much of this volume's focus is on Social Security in the next decade, the issue of whether Social Security will be affordable in the future as the population ages and more people become eligible for benefits is also important. Maintaining a stable replacement rate into the future may create problems when other factors are changing—particularly those that affect our ability to finance future benefits. Just as earlier periods sought an orderly rise in the replacement rate, should we consider a slow decline? If the answer is yes, we might begin to change the benefit formula to generate a smooth transition to lower replacement rates.

The long lead time necessary for a stable transition to any changes in retirement benefits implies that change needs to begin before a crisis is at hand. For purposes of equity, lower benefits might be appropriate even if not essential to bring the system into actuarial balance in the near future. Moreover, future cuts in benefits will affect the working population who might view cuts on current retirees as important for the symbolic purpose of demonstrating shared sacrifice.

But it is also important to recognize that we do not know what the future will hold. Although the balance between working and retiree populations will certainly make benefits less affordable in the future and some downward adjustments will be essential, other factors will also influence future burdens. For example, projecting the rise of wages over time—which is crucial to determine future burdens—is fraught with uncertainty. Imagine attempting in 1935 to estimate the economic circumstances of workers in the 1970s. This uncertainty suggests that it might be both good policy and good politics to make changes for the future in stages rather than attempting, as was done in 1983, to restore the actuarial balance for 75 years. But this means that we should take care that any adjustments in the interim recognize these future issues and begin to pave the way for such changes. The options for change considered below thus attempt to meet two goals: first, to begin to target benefits more effectively to meet current needs and, second, to produce some current and future relief to help with the long-run financing problems that Social Security will face.

SOCIAL SECURITY BENEFITS FORMULA: HOW IT WORKS

Before examining possible changes in Social Security benefits, it is helpful to understand how the Social Security benefit formula works and the basic tenets underlying its formulation. The formula is premised on the notion that lower-income individuals receive a higher percentage of their income back in the form of benefits as compared to higher-income individuals. This creates progressivity in benefit payments and helps offset the regressive nature of the payroll tax on which workers' initial contributions are based. Eligibility for retirement benefits is conditioned on the number of quarters worked. A minimum of 40 quarters is required to receive any benefits.

In turn, benefits for workers are calculated based on three factors: 1) average indexed monthly earnings (AIME), 2) the primary insurance amount (PIA), and 3) adjustments for age of retirement and eligibility status. Historical wages are averaged over an individual's work history and are indexed relative to the national average into the AIME. Indexing is used to account for inflation over a worker's earning years. It creates an earnings record that reflects the value of the individual's earnings relative to the national average earnings in a year close to retirement age.[5]

A worker's AIME then is converted into a primary insurance amount (PIA) using bend points (i.e., income breaks) and replacement rates. Replacement rates signify the percentage of earnings that are reimbursable as benefits, within the given income breaks. For exam-

Table 4.3 CALCULATING PRIMARY INSURANCE AMOUNT IN 1994
(ASSUMING AIME = $3,100)

Replacement Rate		Bend Point (Upper Bound)		Primary Insurance Amount
90 percent	*	$422	=	$379.8
32 percent	*	$2,124 (i.e., the difference between $422 and $2,546)	=	$679.68
15 percent	*	Remaining amount above $2,546	=	$83.25
Total PIA				$1,142.73

ple, in 1994, the monthly bend points were $422 and $2,546, and the replacement rates were 90 percent, 32 percent, and 15 percent. Table 4.3 provides an example of the PIA calculation for a worker reaching age 62 in 1994 with an AIME of $3,100. This person's PIA would be calculated as 90 percent of $422, plus 32 percent of $2,124 (the difference between $422 and $2,546), plus 15 percent of $555 (the difference between $3,100 and $2,546), for a total of $1,142.73. After the year of initial eligibility (age 62 for retired worker benefits), the PIA is increased each year by the increase in the consumer price index (CPI). A worker's PIA is then adjusted further depending on the age of retirement. Dependents' and survivor benefits are estimated from the worker's benefit.[6] The monthly benefits payable to the worker and family members or to the worker's survivors are subject to a maximum family benefit amount.[7] Options for changing many of these provisions are described below.

Lessons from the 1983 Amendments

Many of the policy options proposed in the current debate are reminiscent of the types of changes contained in the Social Security Amendments of 1983. Four characteristics of these changes provide a helpful starting point for generating acceptable solutions for Social Security. First, the 1983 amendments enacted a combination of changes that affected both current and future generations. This is both a fairness and a political issue, and voters will likely be more receptive to possible changes that may adversely affect them if they believe others are sharing in the pain.

Second, to the extent possible, the 1983 reforms were targeted to maintain Social Security's progressivity, protecting poor and near-poor elderly and disabled persons. This is likely to be relevant to the current debate, since concerns about unfair windfalls from the program relate largely to upper-income individuals. Further, as described earlier, Social Security does not uniformly reduce poverty, and a look to the future suggests that low-income persons will remain in need.

Third, because the system encompasses a large portion of the population and affects individuals' long-range plans, major changes that affect future retirees should be phased in slowly. The 1983 amendments, for instance, increased the retirement age, but those changes do not begin to take place until the year 2000. This is particularly important for overall eligibility changes. Individuals make work, savings, and consumption decisions based on their expectations for Social Security, and it would be unfair to change the rules substantially for those within just a few years of retirement.

In addition to these characteristics, decisions made to ensure solvency rely on very long-run projections and need to recognize that despite the increased sophistication of projecting the future, uncertainty still prevails. What appeared to solve the problem in 1983 looks insufficient today. For example, the 1984 Social Security Trustees' report projected that wages would increase at an average rate of about 5.5 percent annually to the year 2000 (Board of Trustees, OASDI Trust Funds 1984). In fact, wages have grown only 4.5 percent a year on average over the last 10 years. This projection led to overly optimistic assumptions about revenue growth into the trust funds, and helps explain why just over a decade later we are again examining options for reform.

Many of the reforms discussed in the subsequent section of this chapter borrow from and improve upon strategies used in the 1983 Social Security Amendments. Like the thrust of those amendments, we stress incremental reforms as politically more feasible and less uncertain as to outcomes, compared to a complete system overhaul. We include here five types of options for reforming Social Security: 1) changes that would result in increased benefits for some recipients, 2) changes that could immediately begin to produce some savings, 3) intermediate changes affecting future beneficiaries and aimed at beginning a long-run transition to a more streamlined system, 4) payroll tax changes, and 5) larger structural options for altering Social Security over the long run. The first three options should be part of any debate concerning entitlements over the next 10 years, while the last two are more of interest for the longer run. Payroll taxes might also be discussed for change in the near term were it not for the current political environment, which makes such a change highly unlikely.

TARGETING OF BENEFITS:
INCREASES FOR SOME BENEFICIARIES

Recognizing the likelihood of a shrinking revenue base should not preclude discussion of expanding benefits for some beneficiaries, although such expansion would likely be funded by cuts elsewhere in the Social Security program. It is important to make the system both more progressive and more equitable. Enlarging the protections for low-income persons in general could be done through Social Security, but a more efficient approach would more likely use the Supplemental Security Income program, which is a federally-funded means tested program for the elderly and disabled which could be expanded (Smeeding 1994). At a minimum, the federal guarantee could be raised to 100 percent of the poverty guidelines, for example.

Several structural issues regarding Social Security do deserve attention, however. Currently, the treatment of traditional and nontraditional families in the calculation of Social Security benefits is inequitable. When the spousal benefit under Social Security was implemented in 1939, the majority of wives did not work. At that time, a one-earner family was considered "traditional." The program was intended to ensure that spouses who are not employed but married to workers covered by Social Security receive benefits even if they do not contribute to the system. In 1992, about three-fifths of women received benefits as wives or widows (Ross and Upp 1993). Employed spouses, on the other hand, pay Social Security taxes but receive no additional benefits if the amount they receive as a dependent is greater than or equal to the amount they are entitled to as workers.

The spousal benefit significantly raises the benefits relative to the contributions for traditional families as compared to households without full-time homemakers (Ross and Upp 1993). Consequently, married couples with full-time homemakers gain at the expense of two-earner households (Ferber 1993). Today, the majority of married women work outside the home, and the "nontraditional" two-earner family has become the norm. Consideration thus needs to be given to proposals to improve the equity of these benefits. But the magnitude of the changes implied and the consequent numbers of winners and losers have served as barriers to finding a politically acceptable solution. More work is needed in this area.

Inequities arise for survivor benefits in a similar manner, but these inequities may present a more tractable set of solutions. Survivor benefits are also inadequate in terms of allowing the survivor to maintain the same standard of living following the death of a spouse. Under the current system, survivors face at least a 33 percent reduction in benefits upon the death of a spouse. However, using the poverty guidelines as indicators of needs for resources, a 20 percent reduction would be more appropriate. This discrepancy likely helps explain why many widows are poor after the death of a spouse, but when still part of a couple, their incomes were above poverty. In addition, loss of pension income and/or depletion of assets to pay for health care needs may also contribute to higher rates of poverty among widows and widowers.

In addition, working widows (or widowers) may experience a larger decline in their benefits than nonworking widows following the death of a spouse.[8] A nonworking woman currently receives 50 percent of her husband's benefit as his dependent. As a couple, therefore, they receive 150 percent of the husband's retirement benefit. If he dies, the widow will now receive 100 percent of the retirement benefit as a survivor. This results in a 33 percent decline from what the family previously received. In contrast, surviving widows of couples in which both spouses had worked receive either their own benefit or their husband's benefit, whichever is larger. In the extreme, if the couple had identical earning patterns, upon the death of the spouse, the widow would experience a 50 percent decline from the previous family benefit. Thus, the survivor in a couple where both were receiving benefits from their own work histories would always experience a greater decline in Social Security benefits than would a survivor who had not worked. Burkhauser and Smeeding (1994) have proposed that widows, regardless of whether in a one-earner or two-earner family, receive a benefit equal to 75 percent of the family benefit upon the death of a spouse. This would represent an improvement in benefits for all survivors, but especially for two-earner couples.

Particularly if Social Security benefits are to be cut elsewhere, some of the savings generated could be used to ease the plight of survivors and of beneficiaries with incomes below poverty.

IMMEDIATE OPTIONS FOR CHANGE

Although there are good reasons to restrict the extent to which benefits for current recipients could be altered, it is important to consider limited options for such changes, both to obtain immediate savings and to require current elderly persons to share in sacrifices. If these changes are used to free up resources for better targeting of either Social Security or related programs, it may be easier to justify them than if savings go toward lowering government spending. At any rate, protections for those with the fewest resources are especially important.

Adjustments to the annual cost-of-living (COLA) update, as well as changes in the taxation of benefits, are potential options that affect both current and future beneficiaries.

Reducing Cost-of-Living Adjustments

Currently, Social Security benefits increase annually to account for changes in the cost of living. These annual updates are based on the consumer price index for wage earners (CPI-W). COLA limitations have been used in the past and are often included in comprehensive reform proposals. Their chief advantage is that they offer relatively large dollar savings for low per capita changes. For example, a one-half percentage point reduction in the COLA for five years would reduce Social Security and Railroad Retirement outlays by about $26 billion (CBO 1995b). But because such a change is broad-based, it affects the most vulnerable beneficiaries as well as those for whom the COLA represents a minor share of income.

In addition to options to directly restrict the COLA, some recent proposals in Congress offer "technical" adjustments to the cost-of-living formula. Most notably, a reduction in the annual CPI has been proposed as a correction for specification errors. By convincing beneficiaries that they are currently receiving a "windfall" from technical errors, removing the windfall by reducing the CPI becomes politically more palatable. Such a change can be billed as merely a technical adjustment. Indeed, the Congressional Budget Resolution for fiscal year 1996 includes such an adjustment, although publicity on the planned budget indicates there will be *no* changes in Social Security. The Resolution actually calls for a 0.4 percentage point reduction in the CPI. This would be a permanent downward adjustment made each year. In practice, this provision would have exactly the same impact as a straight COLA reduction.

Proponents of a technical adjustment argue that the CPI, on which the COLA is based, overestimates inflation. This overestimation occurs because as prices rise, people substitute into less-expensive goods, thus changing the composition of their "market basket." Because the CPI is based on a "fixed market basket," it fails to account for this substitution into cheaper goods and instead results in an increase in the CPI. Moreover, improvements in the quality of goods and services over time are not completely taken into account. According to the Congressional Budget Office (1994a), the extent to which the CPI overestimates inflation ranges between 0.2 and 0.8 percent. But fixing the measurement of the CPI raises complex estimation problems and might take many years to complete. As a consequence, proponents of such a change propose an arbitrary downward adjustment.

One must be careful, however, in offering specification error as a rationale for cutting benefits, because if specification error is the justification for a reduction in the CPI, then an argument could just as well be made in the opposite direction. The CPI-W on which the COLA is based represents the market basket for wage earners. This market basket is very different than that experienced by the elderly, and many would contend that, in fact, it underestimates inflation for persons aged 65 and over. That is, one of the largest components of spending for the elderly as compared to the nonelderly is health care, and the share of consumption applied to health care services in the CPI-W is lower than it would be under an elderly-based CPI. Further, the earlier argument about substitution behavior does not apply as easily to health care, simply because it is more difficult to substitute inexpensive health care services for expensive services and still receive the same quality of care.

There is another more honest, but perhaps less politically palatable, rationale for a decrease in the COLA. That is, we may not be able to afford COLA increases at current rates given the shifting demographic trends. The COLA begins to erode the revenue base because *benefits* increase with prices while *revenues* increase with wages, which have grown more slowly than prices over the past decade. This has led to an erosion in the revenue base at the same time that the retiree-to-worker ratio is rising. This problem is slated to worsen as the retiree-to-worker ratio continues to rise in the next century. To maintain a stable revenue stream under current COLA policies would require either increasing the payroll tax or reducing other parts of the basic benefit structure.

But because of the importance of Social Security to low-income beneficiaries, a COLA reduction would most adversely affect poor beneficiaries. This would also violate the principle of maintaining progressivity. A more progressive approach that deserves serious consideration, with some modifications, has been offered by Senators Bob Kerrey (D.-Neb.) and Alan Simpson (R.-Wyo.) in their Social Security bill (Simpson 1995). Among other changes, their proposal calls for a "modified" COLA, which would set an upper bound on the absolute dollar increase in Social Security benefits in any given year. They suggest setting that amount at the COLA level for beneficiaries receiving benefits at the 30th percentile. For the 70 percent of beneficiaries above that level, the COLA each year would be a fixed dollar amount equal to that of the 30th percentile beneficiary. A COLA would be received by everyone, but would be subject to this upper bound.

While the Kerrey-Simpson approach is a reasonable one, setting the cap at the 30th percentile would adversely affect the elderly poor (see table 4.4). Even a 40th percentile cap would reduce benefits to elderly individuals with incomes below 150 percent of poverty. A more progressive approach might cap the COLA at the 60th percentile of benefits. Consider an example. In 1992, the average benefit for beneficiaries at the 60th percentile was $7,333.[9] If the COLA were 3 percent, the COLA would increase benefits by $220. Thus, a modified COLA would cap annual increases in benefits at $220. Individuals with benefits below the 60th percentile would receive the full COLA (i.e., equal to 3 percent). This approach has the advantage of being progressive, largely affecting higher-income beneficiaries (see table 4.4). Although the approach would raise less revenue than the "modified" COLA set at the 30th percentile, the savings would still be significant—effectively equivalent to about a 0.4 percentage point reduction in the overall COLA. Interestingly, this would achieve the same overall budget reductions recommended by the Congressional Budget Resolution for Fiscal Year 1996, but would distribute these cuts in a more progressive manner.

Taxation of Social Security Benefits

Taxation of Social Security benefits was introduced as part of the Social Security Amendments of 1983, whose broad purpose was to restore actuarial balance to the program. The taxation provision was made even more progressive than the regular income tax by establishing an income threshold below which Social Security is not taxed ($25,000 for single persons and $32,000 for couples). Thus, those with the lowest incomes were unaffected by this provision. And even when reaching the threshold, no more than 50 percent of all Social Security benefits were subjected to taxation. The highest-income beneficiaries were still allowed to deduct half of Social Security benefits from their income for purposes of taxation. In 1995, about 22.9 percent of Social

Table 4.4 PERCENTAGE CHANGE IN SOCIAL SECURITY BENEFITS UNDER ALTERNATIVE FORMULATIONS OF THE MODIFIED COLA, 1992

Income Relative to Poverty	Percentage of Recipients	Percent Change with/Full COLA	Percent Change if Held at 30th Percentile	Percent Change if Held at Median	Percent Change if Held at 60th Percentile
< 100%	12.3	3.0	2.7	2.97	2.99
100–149%	7.8	3.0	2.29	2.78	2.93
150–199%	14.5	3.0	2.09	2.55	2.74
200–249%	19.7	3.0	1.95	2.39	2.57
250–299%	9.7	3.0	1.88	2.33	2.51
300% +	35.8	3.0	1.81	2.23	2.42

Source: The Urban Institute, Washington, D.C.
Note: Estimates based on authors' simulations of 1993 Current Population Survey, March 1993 Supplement.

Security beneficiaries over age 65 are expected to pay some tax on Social Security (U.S. House 1994).

In judging the advisability of taxation of Social Security, a number of principles of taxation can be examined. One major principle is the equal treatment of equals—that is, people with the same incomes should pay the same level of taxes. As discussed in chapter 2, since older Americans have long benefited from the exclusion of this important part of their incomes from taxation, they do not pay as much as younger families in taxes. The expansion of the taxation of Social Security thus actually improves the tax principle of horizontal equity.

Another principle is progressivity—or whether those who have higher ability to pay (usually measured by their incomes) pay a greater share of their incomes in taxes. Again, taxation of Social Security meets this measure of fairness. Moreover, it is a more progressive way to reduce benefits than changing the Social Security benefit formula, for example, because it takes into account all sources of income in determining who should be liable for higher taxes. In that sense, it is a better gauge of ability to pay than if adjustments were made on the basis of Social Security benefits alone. And it is certainly more progressive than across-the-board cuts in cost-of-living adjustments, which constitute another major proposal for Social Security savings.

Taxation of benefits is also consistent with the philosophy of Social Security to *supplement* retirement income for Americans, and to supplement it more generously for those with lower incomes. In fact, taxation of benefits offers an intermediate alternative to full means testing, by providing a mechanism to link benefits received to total income. Unlike means testing, however, taxation does not completely eliminate benefits to high-income beneficiaries, but their benefits could be reduced significantly by taxation depending on the structure of the taxation schedule. Finally, the original legislation on Social Security was silent about whether or not benefits would count as income for purposes of taxation. An Internal Revenue Service ruling—and not legislative intent—excluded this source of income from taxation.

In 1993, the budget reduction bill of Congress and President Bill Clinton extended the taxation of Social Security to include up to 85 percent of benefits for couples with incomes over $44,000 and for individuals with incomes over $34,000. This essentially added a second tier of taxation. For those who are affected, the share of Social Security that counts as income for income tax purposes gradually rises from 50 percent to 85 percent. Thus, even the highest-income beneficiaries are allowed to shelter 15 percent of their benefits from taxation—still giving them an advantage over younger families with similar levels of income. Only about 13 percent of elderly beneficiaries are affected by this second tier (U.S. House 1995).

The additional taxation enacted in 1993 had another important element: these new revenues were dedicated to the Medicare Hospital Insurance trust fund to help improve its financial health. Thus, every dollar that higher-income beneficiaries pay goes to help pay benefits to Medicare beneficiaries. Effectively, this is a way to make the Medicare program more progressive as well, without generating new administrative structures to do so.[10]

Recent bills have been proposed in Congress to roll back the 1993 expansion. Elimination of the 1993 legislation would deprive the Medicare trust fund of needed revenues and accelerate its fiscal crisis.[11] Thus, any assessment of the value of rescinding this legislation should also consider the impact on the Medicare program because of the direct linkage between the two programs. Ironically, this expanded taxation of benefits is consistent with the types of sacrifices that Americans need to be asked to make in the future to ensure that Social Security and Medicare fulfill their promises over time. Repeal of this provision would send a contradictory signal to Americans about changes that are required for the future. In fact, one important option for changing Social Security would be to further expand the taxation of benefits. Such an expansion could be accomplished either by lowering the income thresholds or increasing the percentage of benefits subject to tax.[12]

A more extreme move would be total elimination of the income thresholds. Estimates by the Bipartisan Commission on Entitlements and Tax Reform (1995) found that taxation of all Social Security benefits with no thresholds would increase revenue by .28 percent of covered payroll, or 13 percent of what would be needed for long-run solvency of the system.[13] Simulations by Pattison and Harrington (1993) found that elimination of the thresholds would mean that 60 percent of beneficiary families would pay taxes on their benefits. This provision would not affect families with incomes in the lowest two quintiles (the bottom 40 percent of the elderly), because their incomes are too low to generate any tax payments. Taxes would increase on average by $667 per household, which would be equivalent to a family losing 5.1 percent of their Social Security benefits.[14] Eliminating the thresholds would burden middle-income families the most, resulting in as much as a 2 percent increase in taxes. Because most of their benefits are already subject to tax, high-income families would be unaffected on the margin by an elimination of the threshold.

The second way to alter the taxation of benefits formula would be to raise the percentage of benefits included in gross taxable income. This is termed the "inclusion ratio."[15] The Congressional Budget Office (1995b) has considered several combinations of changes in the thresholds or the inclusion ratio. For example, subjecting all benefits to full taxation would raise $98 billion over five years. About half that amount could be raised by leaving the 85 percent threshold in place and subjecting everyone else to taxation at 50 percent. Keeping the current lower thresholds at $25,000 and $32,000 but subjecting everyone above that to an 85 percent inclusion ratio would raise only $4 billion over five years.

INTERMEDIATE REFORM OPTIONS

A number of reform options that would retain Social Security largely in its present form but make changes for future beneficiaries could generate substantial savings over time. As a broader debate begins concerning the long-run prospects for Social Security, it may be desirable to begin slowly implementing such changes. Such efforts may help to position the program for the future and could remove some of the pressures from Medicare and the long-term care portion of Medicaid. Thus, these efforts can be considered intermediate in the sense that they can bridge the gap between altering entitlement policies today and relieving future pressures.

We consider here two areas of such possible reforms: first, changing the benefit formula to increase its progressivity; and second, raising the age of eligibility or at least speeding up the existing schedule.

Changing the Benefit Formula

To change the Social Security benefit formula, either the replacement rate or bend points (i.e., wage thresholds where the replacement rates change) could be changed. These would only affect new retirees as their benefits are set in place. Any changes in the benefit formula ought to be carefully considered with respect to their effects on progressivity and the elderly poor, and they should be coordinated with COLA or taxation of benefit changes. Too much emphasis on making changes progressive without examining the combined impacts of separate changes could also lead to unintended consequences.

CHANGING THE REPLACEMENT RATE

One way to lower benefits is to change the rate at which wages are replaced by benefits (i.e., the replacement rate). As described above, currently the replacement rates are 90 percent, 32 percent, and 15 percent. These rates, however, should be changed only in a manner that both protects the progressivity of the system and pays special attention to poor beneficiaries. For example, while changing all three replacement rates would maintain the relative progressivity in the system between high and low wage earners, it would reduce (as a percentage of total income) the already limited income of the poor more than the income of wealthy Social Security recipients. A recent estimate by the Congressional Budget Office (1995b) found that lowering all three replacement rates to 87.3 percent, 31.0 percent, and 14.6 percent would have achieved essentially a uniform 3 percent reduction in benefits of newly eligible workers. But because the poor rely more heavily on Social Security as a percentage of income, this would represent a higher percentage reduction in their incomes. The across-the-board reductions in the replacement rates would save $6.3 billion over a five-year period if implemented in 1996.

Focusing change on the top replacement rates of 32 percent and 15 percent would better protect those with low incomes, but altering the second replacement rate would still affect most beneficiaries. That is, Cohen and Beedon (1994) found that reducing the second replacement rate would affect nearly 83 percent of beneficiaries. Thus, the most desirable change in terms of progressivity would be to concentrate most of the reduction on the top replacement rate. This would limit the revenues saved, but it would better meet the principles outlined previously. Moreover, it is not desirable to lower the third replacement rate to zero. Although this would certainly lower benefits to high-income earners and increase progressivity, it would likely not be politically feasible, since it would concentrate the impact on a relatively small number of beneficiaries. Such an action also begins to move away from the principle of linking benefits and contributions. Finally, even this dramatic change would not significantly improve the solvency of the trust fund (Cohen and Beedon 1994).

CHANGING THE BEND POINTS

An alternative to changing the replacement rates is to alter the "bend points." In 1994, the bend points were $422 and $2,545, and represented the wage thresholds where the replacement rates change. Lowering the bend points would subject a smaller portion of average wages to a larger replacement rate. Because these bend points increase annually with inflation, one obvious way to lower benefits is to reduce the rate at which one or both of these bend points rises each year. This would result in a decline in the level of real benefits over time. Again, changing the upper bend point is more consistent with the principle of progressivity and protection of the poor. An alternative would be to add a third bend point and apply an even lower replacement rate (as suggested by Senators Kerrey and Simpson [Simpson 1995]).

Changing Age of Eligibility for Full Benefits

When Social Security was enacted in 1935, women reaching age 65 were expected to live another 13.4 years and men were expected to live for an additional 11.9 years. Life expectancies have increased significantly since then. In 1990, a woman reaching age 65 is expected to live, on average, 19 years, and for men the number is 15 years (Board of Trustees, Federal OASDI Trust Funds 1995).

Recognizing this increase in life expectancy, the 1983 amendments raised the age of eligibility for full Social Security benefits. The Normal Retirement Age (NRA) will gradually rise at a rate of two months per year beginning for people age 57 and younger in 1995. The NRA will be age 66 for people age 52 in 1995 and will remain at age 66 for persons between age 40 and 52 in 1995. It will then begin to rise again by two-month increments starting with persons who are age 40 and under in 1995, until it reaches age 67 for persons currently under age 36. To protect early retirees, it will remain possible to retire at 62, but benefits will be adjusted downward to be actuarially equivalent to retiring at age 67. Thus, if the age of retirement does not change, individuals who retire before their NRA will receive lower benefits in the future than they would under current rules.

Over the last decade, life expectancies have continued to rise and are expected to increase even further in the next century. Women retiring in 2020 at age 65 are expected to live an additional 20.2 years and men another 16.5 years. Thus, the changes enacted in 1983 do not fully adjust for the greater expected number of years that people will draw benefits. It is therefore reasonable to consider a further increase in the Normal Retirement Age.

One of the main criticisms of raising the retirement age, however, is that this may penalize individuals with moderate disabilities who do not qualify for Social Security disability but for whom longer work lives are not viable options. Low-wage persons whose jobs are physically demanding are particularly at risk, suggesting that this policy change may be regressive.

Currently, stringent disability requirements make it difficult to receive such benefits. If the retirement age were increased, it might be appropriate to lessen disability requirements for those nearing age 65, to ensure that they will not be penalized if they are unable to extend their work lives. (Problems with the rapid expansion of disability claimants might be worsened by such a policy, however.) In addition, expanding opportunities for part-time work and changing the attitudes of both employers and employees ought to be sought as part of a broad strategy to alter the outlook for older workers in the United States.

Changing the age of eligibility is a popular option among many reform plans currently under consideration in Congress. The recent proposal by Senators Kerrey and Simpson (Simpson 1995) would accelerate the move toward 67 as the full retirement age and shortens considerably the phase-in period. The proposal would also increase the retirement age further to age 70 for people currently under age 29, and would tie benefits to life expectancy thereafter. This provision of their larger proposal is expected to address nearly half of the long-run shortfall in the program. But age 70 represents a substantial increase in retirement age, and there is little evidence to suggest that Americans will willingly push back the date of retirement to such a degree. Certainly less-dramatic changes can and should be considered, such as accelerating the timetable for raising the NRA to age 67 and then continuing to expand it to age 68.[16]

RAISING PAYROLL TAXES

Currently, the Social Security system is self-financed through a payroll tax, paid by both employees and employers. The tax rate for Old-Age and Survivors Insurance (OASI) is 5.6 percent each for both the employee and employer, and the Disability Insurance (DI) tax is .6 percent each. The rates have been raised substantially since the inception of the program when they were set at one-half of a percent for the employee and employer (for OASI only). The most recent increase in the payroll tax resulted from the 1983 amendments, with the last set of changes in that legislation implemented in 1990.

Although increased payroll taxes could be added to the list of short-run options, such changes more realistically belong in the category of long-run options for improving Social Security solvency.[17] Even then, relying entirely on the payroll tax to bring the system into long-run actuarial balance would not be advisable. The current shortfall in the trust fund is projected to be 2.17 percent of payroll, meaning that the payroll tax would have to rise 2.17 percentage points to bring the trust fund into actuarial balance. This would place all of the burden on current workers (i.e., future beneficiaries). Smaller changes, on the other hand, could provide some funds to improve solvency. Whereas some believe these rates are already too high and place an excessive burden on workers, especially low-income workers, these arguments overlook the fact that many low-income individuals are protected by the Earned Income Tax Credit which was explicitly designed to ease the payroll tax burden. Moreover, compared to other countries, the U.S. population is not overtaxed (Steuerle 1992).

Of greater concern would be the extent to which raising the payroll tax would worsen, rather than improve, intergenerational concerns. This would occur because we would be forcing current workers to pay more now for perhaps fewer benefits in the future. Also, coupled with earlier recommendations for raising the retirement age and changing the benefits formula, an increase in the payroll tax would disproportionately place the burden of improving solvency on the younger generation. Again, this suggests delaying any increase in the payroll tax.

There is an additional caveat associated with raising the payroll tax now and having the trust fund balances rise. Such an approach assumes that these funds are actually saved. In reality, the trust fund is used to purchase government debt and is not actually put aside for the future. So when the baby boomers retire, this debt will have to be repaid—possibly through further increases in taxes at that time. On the other hand, if any rise in the payroll tax were invested in the private sector, a better case could be made. That is, another proposal on the table for Social Security is to invest some part of the trust fund in private securities both to receive a higher return on the funds, which are now in excess of $450 billion (Board of Trustees, Federal OASDI Trust Funds 1995), and to keep the trust funds from being used to finance current government spending. But private investment of the trust fund is, at best, only a partial solution. Private investment is a more appealing option if the payroll tax rises in the near-term, since that would keep the fund balances high and generate greater returns. This would ironically pair one option (private investment) popular with conservatives with one (higher taxes) very unpopular.

MAJOR STRUCTURAL CHANGES

Proposals for major structural changes in Social Security have varied little over the years. Generally, such proposals would either scale back the program substantially or move parts of it to private pension arrangements. Essentially, these major restructuring proposals focus on separating the two primary functions of Social Security: poverty prevention and public pension. These proposals either explicitly provide separate roles for each function or they just cover the poverty prevention portion and rely on individuals to save further for retirement on their own.

Means Testing

Most proposals to restructure the poverty prevention portion of Social Security focus on means testing (i.e., making eligibility dependent on income). Advocates of means testing, whose premise is that high-income people do not *need* Social Security benefits, argue that the original goal of Social Security was to provide a floor of protection, which can be done without subsidizing the income of people who have more than adequate incomes without Social Security.

A means-tested program poses a number of disadvantages, however. From a political perspective, means testing connotes "welfare programs," which at present are extremely unpopular and often come with stringent caps or other mechanisms to limit costs. Means testing thus could undermine the political consensus supporting Social Security. Further, participation rates are often low in welfare programs because of the stigma of being on welfare and the inadequacy of benefits in many of these programs. Consequently, many of those in need would also fail to be helped by such a program.

Most important, savings from means testing Social Security depend heavily on the income level on which eligibility is phased out. Social Security benefits are vital to middle-income as well as poor elderly and disabled persons, which thus argues for a moderate income eligibility cutoff. Moreover, to move from a universal program to a severely means-tested one seems unnecessarily restrictive. But, if the income eligibility levels are high, such a program might not solve Social Security's long-run solvency problems. What, then, is the appropriate level? For example, if Social Security and SSI were eliminated and replaced with a means-tested program, we estimate that it would cost about $60 billion just to bring everyone up to the Census poverty lines in 1992. If Social Security were set so as to protect both the poor and near-poor elderly with incomes up to 150 percent of the poverty threshold, the costs would be quite high—over $100 billion, or nearly half of current OASI expenditures. And setting the cutoffs at a level to protect those with higher incomes, say to 200 percent of poverty, would add another million elderly people and thus require even more resources.

As in most means-tested programs, there would be perverse incentives at the margin unless benefits were slowly phased out. That is, if each dollar of other income reduces benefits by a dollar, individuals would be discouraged from attempting to raise their incomes because of high implicit taxes or penalties from earning more. Slower phase-outs and income disregards further increase the costs of the program, however. For instance, a means-tested program could simply expand upon the existing Supplemental Security Income program which now serves very low-income elderly and disabled persons. Under SSI, wages are effectively subjected to a 50 percent tax, and other income is disregarded up to a certain level before benefits are reduced. These adjustments improve the behavioral incentives of programs but raise costs and implicitly expand eligibility.

Demogrants

An alternative to means testing would be to guarantee *every* beneficiary a *minimum* level of benefits that would not vary by income. This minimum payment is called a "demogrant" and is a common feature of Social Security systems in Europe. The advantage to a demogrant is that it retains the notion of universality. It is not means tested, avoiding the complicated administrative structures and stigma of a welfare benefit. The expectation would be that this would serve as the base for retirement, and individuals would then either voluntarily or through a required program invest privately to supplement this benefit.

The disadvantage is that a demogrant system, if created to be generous enough to protect those with no other sources of income, would be very expensive. That is, if it were set high enough to bring individuals to or above the poverty line, that same amount would be given to all workers or perhaps all beneficiaries. Many of those with high incomes or still in the labor force would receive much higher grants than they need, while others would receive barely adequate subsidies. The benefits would be more targeted than today, but not enough so as to generate large savings. That is, a demogrant at or near the poverty line would use nearly as many resources as the current Social Security program, so there would be little left to return to individuals to invest privately or to use for savings.

For example, if current Social Security expenditures were distributed based on a demogrant to current beneficiaries (including dependents and survivors), each individual would receive approximately $7,757 annually.[18] This represents just over 100 percent of the federal poverty level for a single-person family. Thus, if the poverty level were the standard of adequacy, few savings would be generated. While the simplicity of a demogrant is appealing, it does not directly address the solvency issue unless it is set low enough to generate savings, nor does it improve most of the current inequities.

Privatization

Many major restructuring options propose to privatize the pension portion of Social Security. Most of these plans maintain public contributions for life and disability insurance, recognizing the acute problems of adverse selection and moral hazard. These proposals emphasize private investment of funds in excess of some minimum benefit (presumably set under a demogrant or means-tested basic tier, for example). Advocates of privatization believe it will reduce the disincentive effects of Social Security on national savings and may in fact increase total savings (Weaver 1993). They further argue that investment of Social Security revenues in the private sector would raise the rate of return received by beneficiaries as compared to Treasury Securities and would allow returns on investments to be "saved" in a way that our current public pension system does not.

Privatization proposals are usually offered under two alternative structures that differ depending upon who controls the investment decisions: the government or the individual. Both structures require mandatory payments, and each option has its own set of pitfalls. Permitting individuals to make their own decisions has the appeal of stressing individual responsibility. Further, individuals might become more aware of what their public retirement benefits will look like and hence supplement them. But, if individuals are allowed to invest on their own, they could face lower returns than expected. People—especially those with limited information and experience in this area—may not invest wisely (Swoboda 1995; CBO 1994b). Further, higher returns come with higher risks. Individuals who invest in risky assets and then lose could experience a lower return than would have occurred even with the very protected federal securities

(Bosworth 1995). But if investments are too conservative, returns may be very low as well. Experience with 401k plans, for example, suggests that many Americans invest these pension dollars very conservatively and hence are not getting high returns. Finally, individual decision making carries high administrative costs as plans seek to attract investors, for example.

On the other hand, if the government were to invest citizens' monies for them, risk could be spread more evenly across individuals by virtue of experienced money managers making these decisions. Problems could arise, however, if this huge supply of funds for private investment led to conflicts between investment decisions and claims by special interest groups. Various lobbying groups could end up competing for some share of the funds, generating a political free-for-all (Weaver 1990).

Beyond these concerns, the effect of privatization on national savings is also uncertain. Currently, the trust fund is invested in government bonds (essentially representing IOUs), which do not increase total savings; in fact, some contend the bonds crowd out funds by raising interest rates. If these funds were invested privately, but the government continued to run a deficit, someone would still have to purchase the public debt. This would leave national savings unchanged (Boskin 1986). The only way for savings to rise would be for the government to begin to actually run a surplus. Further, if this were combined with a truly means-tested program, there could be large incentives not to save additional monies for retirement (Bosworth 1995), or not to save additional amounts if workers assumed that this portion of Social Security represented all the "supplemental" savings necessary.

Most importantly, privatization would not overcome the demographic constraints. As stated earlier, given the nature of the system, there will be more retirees to workers in the future, which will lower the rate of return for future beneficiaries. If some resources are directed to redistribution and disability protections, the remainder of funds available for private investment will still be limited, affecting retirees in similar ways. The windfalls of the past are not available to be privately invested.

In reality, there is great uncertainty surrounding the potential effects of privatization of Social Security, not only regarding the distribution of benefits and the effect on overall savings (CBO 1994b) but in terms of privatization's impact on the long-run solvency of the trust fund. A major restructuring of the system, while appealing to some, would require an increase, rather than a decline, in expenditures over the foreseeable future as one system is being phased out and another introduced (Steuerle and Bakija 1994). This dual system would also likely impose additional administrative costs. Since covering the poor adequately and developing a whole new private pension system would be costly, this solution might therefore fail to appease Congress, which is looking for ways to reduce and not expand expenditures associated with entitlements over time.

CONCLUSIONS

Social Security has been very successful in helping to raise the standard of living of older Americans and persons with disabilities. It now accounts for a higher share of income for persons over age 65 than it did in 1962 (Grad 1994). The buying power of seniors has improved, and rates of poverty have declined.

Nevertheless, the progress of the elderly relative to the young in our society has created somewhat of a backlash. The very success of Social Security has led to calls for reducing the generosity of the system even for current beneficiaries. The evidence does seem to indicate that as a society, we have done a reasonably comprehensive job of sharing economic growth with elderly and disabled persons outside the economic mainstream. But there is considerable room for debate about exactly where older Americans stand economically relative to the young. Moreover, it would be a mistake to either attribute all of the narrowing of economic well-being between the two to the burdens that Social Security places on the young or to use that as the major reason for cutting benefits.

Finally, it is likely to be more realistic to advocate future changes that gradually alter Social Security rather than proposals that rapidly reduce benefits in the near term. Older Americans in their 50s and 60s have already made substantial decisions about retirement, savings and other activities based on expected benefits. Adjusting to change takes time; thus, even if benefits seem too generous, proposals for change must be balanced against these constraints.

When examining the goals of reform, it is important to keep in mind why Social Security enjoys widespread support from all age groups. Social Security is universal in nature. Eligibility is based solely on age and number of quarters of labor force participation, and there is a highly visible relationship between taxes paid and benefits received in the form of retirement, life, and disability annuities. This universality of Social Security is very different from means-tested programs (i.e., in which eligibility is based on having limited resources) intended to help the poor. These programs have low participation rates and income eligibility thresholds that are often well below the poverty line. Privatization proposals hold some additional promise, but there is not yet sufficient consensus to radically restructure the program at present, particularly given the current partisan debate over Social Security and its place in the federal budget. The split in the Social Security Advisory Commission over this issue in the first half of 1995 suggests that more discussion is needed before a final decision on such an approach can be made even outside the political arena (Rich 1995). Instead, incremental reforms should be addressed that improve solvency, but at the same time, better target benefits and achieve some short-run savings. It is furthermore reasonable to consider whether some reductions in Social Security should be undertaken to shift resources to the health care entitlements that also serve the elderly. Proposed changes in those programs are the subject of the next two chapters.

Notes

1. The term *progressivity* is more often applied to taxation, and then in the opposite direction—requiring higher tax contributions as a share of income from those with higher incomes.

2. The indexing error from the 1972 amendments became apparent when rates of inflation exceeded wage growth in the mid-1970s. Efforts to correct this problem led to the 1977 amendments. But the correction has also proven to be controversial, leading to the so-called notch problem. A vocal group of retirees born after 1916 who were subject to the correction noted that their benefits were lower than benefits for similar persons born in 1915 or 1916. Essentially, they want to have the same error in their favor that the earlier retirees received. A good discussion of this issue can be found in a study by the National Academy of Social Insurance (1988).

3. A number of analysts have proposed, instead, that the Supplemental Security Income program—which is directly targeted to those with low incomes—be expanded, rather than making changes in Social Security specifically.

4. Making broad comparisons of this sort requires a number of assumptions about equivalence that are subject to considerable debate. For example, most analysts agree that we ought to adjust incomes for differences in family size in comparing across different demographic groups, but there is no consensus about what the exact adjustment should be. Showing income per family tends to understate well-being for the old (since family sizes are smaller for those over age 65), but per capita numbers are biased in exactly the opposite direction. Thus, there can be disagreement about exactly how the elderly compare to the younger population, but it would be very difficult to argue

that the elderly are substantially better off than their younger counterparts, as some have claimed.

5. The indexing year is the second year before the year in which the worker attains age 62 or when he or she becomes disabled or dies. Earnings after the indexing year are counted at their nominal value.

6. Benefits are also reduced for those whose earnings exceed an annual limit. An increase in that limit has been proposed in the Republicans' Contract with America and passed the House of Representatives in the spring of 1995.

7. The maximum benefit for retired-worker families or survivor families varies by primary insurance amount (PIA) level, between 150 and 188 percent of the PIA.

8. Although this problem affects many more women than men, the issue is essentially the same if the wife dies first. Men generally have somewhat higher incomes than women living alone, however.

9. The figure of $7,333 represents an estimate using the Current Population Survey and may vary from estimates using Social Security Administration records.

10. Dedication of these revenues to the Medicare HI Trust Fund also constitutes an example of the important linkages across elderly entitlement programs.

11. The Treasury Department estimates that this provision will add $15 billion to the Medicare Trust Fund over the next 5 years, and $48.5 billion between 1995 and 2005.

12. Actually, because the thresholds are not indexed for inflation, they will decline in real terms over time without any further legislative changes. Since 1984, the absence of indexation of the thresholds has increased the number of individuals subject to taxation from 8.4 to 20 percent (Pattison and Harrington 1993).

13. Such a dramatic change is likely to represent a long-term option for reform, rather than one considered in the near term.

14. This estimate was made prior to the 1993 expansion, so it overstates the impact.

15. The inclusion ratio was designed to treat the taxation of Social Security in a manner similar to the taxation of private pensions. Whereas the employee's contribution to Social Security is paid for out of income that is already taxed, the employer's contribution is not included in gross earnings and therefore is not part of taxable income (Boskin 1986). Therefore, at least half of Social Security benefits are tax-free. Thus, when benefits were initially taxed in 1983, a 50 percent inclusion rate was used. More recently, an 85 percent inclusion rate has been justified as being consistent with the current taxation of pensions (U.S. House 1994).

16. Accelerating the timetable for raising the NRA to age 67 and then expanding it to age 68 was put forth as a possible option by the Kerry-Danforth Entitlement Commission (Kerry and Danforth 1995) and was projected to eliminate about a quarter of the long-range financing problem.

17. Here again is an area where linkage with Medicare is very important. Any near-term increases in the payroll tax might be reserved for Medicare.

18. It is likely that a smaller grant to dependents would be offered, but this example is meant simply to illustrate the issue.

Chapter Five

MEDICARE

Issues facing the Medicare program differ along a number of important dimensions as compared to Social Security. The nature of the benefit received from Medicare is quite different, in that beneficiaries get benefits "in kind" in the form of insurance coverage. Medicare payments go toward the costs of acute medical care and not directly to beneficiaries. This generates several further distinctions as opposed to the way Social Security operates. First, it means that the benefits are "lumpy"—that is, everyone receives the same basic insurance package. Second, these in-kind benefits are described as coverage for certain types of medical care, leading to automatic changes in the cost of providing the benefit when either the expense of providing the service rises or the standards for treating medical problems signal an increase in the exact treatments that need to be rendered. Third, because Medicare dollars do not go directly to beneficiaries, Medicare is viewed as a program that can more readily be cut as part of budget balancing efforts.

Because of the standard benefit package, the Medicare program effectively treats the elderly and disabled more as a homogeneous group than does Social Security. When passed in 1965, the Medicare program grandfathered in all persons over the age of 65, granting each person the same benefits.[1] Only beginning in 1968 were beneficiaries required to be eligible for some type of Social Security benefit, either as a worker, spouse, or survivor. But even then, those eligible for the minimum Social Security benefits received the same insurance protection as persons receiving the highest Social Security payments. Thus, unlike Social Security, where benefits vary depending upon contributions and other factors, once a person becomes eligible for Medicare there are no distinctions across benefits.[2] This has led some critics of Medicare to argue that it is not a progressive program. But that ignores the financing side of the equation. Because the benefit package is constant, beneficiaries with high wages during their working years pay much more for a flat benefit. In the case of Social

Security, benefits rise with contributions, albeit at a declining rate. In that sense, Medicare constitutes an even more progressive program above a certain minimum.

There are also practical reasons for establishing just one basic insurance benefit. Unlike Social Security, whereby the value of the public benefit is easy to vary in small increments according to a formula, it is more cumbersome to offer partial insurance coverage or benefits differentiated by income. Additional mechanisms would be necessary to administer such changes, complicating Medicare. Over time, these practical concerns have effectively limited the types of options available for changing the program to make it vary with income. As national attention has focused more on entitlements, however, dramatic options for altering Medicare along these lines are being given more serious attention.

The second issue that is dramatically different for Medicare as opposed to Social Security is the natural tendency for the program costs to rise each year even though the defined benefits are unchanged. This would be less of an issue if the benefits under discussion were not subject either to the rates of health care price inflation we have seen in recent years or to the technological advances that have made health care for everyone more expensive and more effective. Although new technology and greater expectations about necessary treatments can be argued to have changed what beneficiaries receive under Medicare, the benefit package itself has technically not varied.[3] But these promised benefits have become much more expensive over time. This reality has made the urgency of dealing with the program greater than for Social Security, with exhaustion of the Hospital Insurance trust fund projected to occur by 2002 (Board of Trustees, Federal HI Trust Fund 1995). But the fact that increases in Medicare expenditures are so tied to the costs of medical care also makes solutions more dependent on exogenous influences such as technology and the ways that health care is delivered. Alternatively, some analysts have begun to explicitly raise the issue of whether Medicare should continue as a defined benefit program or shift into more of a defined contribution mode in which Medicare would guarantee only a given level of contributions each year toward the cost of health care.[4]

The third distinction mentioned at the outset of this chapter is that, correctly or not, many legislators regard Medicare as a less-crucial program than Social Security. Promises of keeping Social Security off limits in the federal deficit reduction debate have not kept Medicare off limits in the same way. In part, this likely reflects a perceived heirarchy between these two programs. Social Security has been in existence longer, and it offers cash benefits that recipients can use for any purpose including medical care. Moreover, since beneficiaries receive services and the government sends payments to the providers of those services, legislators often contend that it is possible to cut payments to doctors and hospitals while maintaining services. And, indeed, many of the cuts in Medicare in recent years have done exactly that. The Budget Resolution outlining plans for the federal budget in fiscal year 1996 calls for over $270 billion in savings from Medicare while doing little to change Social Security.[5] Thus, the perception of Medicare as an easier program to cut has taken hold.[6]

These three important distinctions between Medicare and Social Security represent key areas for investigating options for change. Before considering how Medicare might be modified over time, however, the next section examines a number of issues that influence how we should view Medicare. That section is followed by a general discussion of options for reform and the principles that should be at play in such a consideration. Finally, we consider a number of specific reform options and their likely impact on Medicare.

THE IMPORTANCE OF MEDICARE TO OLDER AMERICANS

Medicare has contributed substantially to the well-being of America's oldest and most disabled citizens. It is the largest public health care program in the United States, providing the major source of insurance for acute care for the elderly and disabled. Its administrative costs are low—constituting only about 2 to 4 percent of total spending—and it is popular with both its beneficiaries and the general population. Moreover, relative to total health care costs, Medicare has done rather well in the 1980s and early 1990s, growing more slowly on a per capita basis as compared to health care spending covered by private insurance (Moon and Zuckerman 1995) (see figure 5.1). Although the common perception seems to be that Medicare is growing much faster than private insurance (Freudenheim 1995; Hage and Black 1995), a careful look at the data suggests that in the recent past that has not been the case, particularly when the comparisons are made using per capita numbers from a consistent database, and are limited to services covered both by Medicare and private insurance.

Medicare is divided into two parts.[7] Hospital Insurance (Part A) covers hospital, skilled nursing facility (SNF), and home health care services. Hospital and SNF care are limited within a given spell of

Figure 5.1 PER CAPITA GROWTH RATES OF SERVICES COVERED BY BOTH
MEDICARE AND PRIVATE INSURANCE, 1976–93

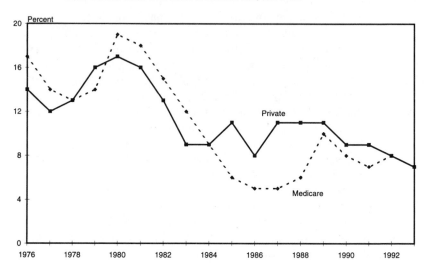

Source: Moon and Zuckerman 1995.

illness, and are subject after 60 days of hospital and 20 days of SNF
care to substantial coinsurance. Home health care, intended to be for
skilled needs, requires no beneficiary contributions. A limited hos-
pice benefit is also available under Part A. Supplementary Medical
Insurance (Part B) covers physician services, outpatient hospital services, and other ambulatory care for those who wish to enroll. Physician services and most of the other Part B services require a 20
percent coinsurance payment and a $100 deductible. Spending on
these services and projected rates of growth through the year 2000
are detailed in table 5.1. Hospital services, although very large, are
projected to grow much more slowly than spending on home health
care, for example.

Part A is mainly funded by payroll tax contributions of workers and
by a part of the revenues collected from the taxation of Social Security
benefits. Beneficiaries aged 65 and older are automatically eligible if
they are eligible for Social Security benefits. Part B is funded by a
combination of general revenues and premium contributions from
beneficiaries. Those eligible for Part A can choose to enroll in Part B,
which is voluntary. About 98 percent of the elderly do so.

One of the difficulties in considering how to cut the Medicare program is that, in some areas, Medicare's coverage is much less com-

Table 5.1 PROJECTIONS OF MEDICARE SPENDING, FISCAL YEARS
1995 AND 2000

Component of Medicare Spending	Outlays (in billions)		Projected Average Annual Rate of Growth (%)
	1995	2000	
Part A: Hospital Insurance:			
Total outlays[a]	113.6	172.5	8.7
Total benefits:	112.0	170.7	8.8
Hospitals	79.0	104.8	5.8
HMOs	7.4	19.2	21.1
Hospice	1.9	4.7	20.0
Home health	14.7	26.2	12.2
Skilled nursing facilities	9.0	15.7	11.7
Part B: Supplementary Medical Insurance:			
Total outlays[a]	67.6	119.4	12.1
Total benefits:	65.8	117.1	12.2
Physicians	32.8	52.3	9.8
Durable medical equipment	2.9	5.7	14.2
Laboratories	4.7	8.2	11.6
Outpatient hospital	10.4	20.5	14.4
HMOs	6.8	16.7	19.6
Other	8.0	13.7	11.2
Total Outlays	181.1	291.9	10.0
Total premiums	20.1	27.3	6.4
Net Outlays	161.1	264.6	10.4

Source: CBO 1995b.
a. Outlays include both benefit payments and administrative costs.

prehensive than private insurance. For example, Medicare does not provide coverage for prescription drugs, and its mental health benefits are quite limited. A high hospital deductible ($716 in 1995) and lack of "stop-loss" protections[8] also represent program inadequacies.

Because Medicare leaves a number of gaps in coverage, a market for private supplemental insurance—often referred to as Medigap—has grown up around Medicare. About three out of four seniors have some form of private supplemental insurance, divided about equally between insurance purchased privately or offered as part of a retirement benefits package (Chulis et al. 1993). Retiree health insurance is at least partially subsidized by employers, reducing the costs that beneficiaries must pay. This type of supplemental insurance often is more comprehensive as well, paying not only the coinsurance and deductibles required under Medicare but also often including additional benefits such as prescription drug coverage. Those who must pay the full costs of supplemental insurance usually pay at least $800 per year in premiums for the most common plans.

Low-income persons may have gaps in Medicare covered by the Medicaid program, which is targeted on those who are eligible for income support under the Supplemental Security Income program and those who have very high medical expenses that leave them with low incomes after accounting for medical costs.[9] In addition to the standard coverage under Medicaid, a program for Qualified Medicare Beneficiaries (QMB) was added in 1989 to have Medicaid pay Medicare premiums and cost sharing for persons up to the poverty line who do not receive traditional Medicaid benefits.[10] And those with incomes between 100 percent and 120 percent of the poverty line are eligible under a related program for assistance with Part B premiums. This expansion has had a considerable impact on the elderly, raising participation in Medicaid to 11.9 percent in 1991 for persons aged 65 and older, as compared to 7.6 percent in 1987 (Chulis et al. 1993). Participation in this program remains a problem, however. For example, only about 41 percent of all those eligible are now covered by the QMB program (Neumann et al. 1994).

Even with Medicare, Medicaid, and private insurance, persons over age 65 face substantial out-of-pocket expenses for acute-care services. Total spending on behalf of elderly noninstitutionalized persons averaged about $6,930 per capita in 1994, and $1,382 was paid directly by individuals. To that should be added the amount that individuals must pay in premiums for Medicare and supplemental insurance— another $1,137, bringing total costs borne by an average elderly person to about $2,519. These amounts are shown in table 5.2, disaggregated by type of health service. As described in chapter 2, these costs consume 21 percent of the incomes of a typical person over age 65.

How should we interpret these high rates of health care spending by elderly persons? Is spending on health care out of line for the elderly as compared with the rest of the population? Average acute-care spending for persons over age 65 is about 3.8 times as high as for those under age 65 (Lefkowitz and Monheit 1991). A number of critical factors boost the costs of acute health care spending for older persons: the higher acute- and chronic-care needs of older persons, demands on services at the end of life, the aging of the population, the role of technology, and the special needs of long-term care. And since the elderly disproportionately use long-term care services, the ratio would likely be even higher if these services were taken into account as well. These constraints need to be considered when assessing how Medicare should change over time.

Table 5.2 AVERAGE HEALTH CARE COSTS FOR NONINSTITUTIONALIZED ELDERLY BY AGE, 1994

	All Elderly ($)	Aged 65–69 ($)	Aged 70–74 ($)	Aged 75–79 ($)	Aged 80–84 ($)	Aged 85+ ($)
Insurance Premium Contributions:						
Employment-related insurance	177	253	180	108	124	94
Individual private insurance	502	359	501	671	601	550
Medicare Part B	458	466	462	452	448	438
Subtotal	1,137	1,078	1,143	1,231	1,173	1,082
Out-of-Pocket:						
Physician services	419	353	365	488	646	390
Hospital services	180	87	138	175	386	427
Prescribed medicine	246	209	233	288	323	234
Dental	131	158	146	113	85	73
Durable medical equipment	41	22	43	42	80	59
Vision	38	40	41	38	34	22
Home health care	327	103	155	213	742	1,495
Subtotal	1,382	972	1,121	1,357	2,296	2,700
Total	2,519	2,051	2,264	2,588	3,469	3,782

Source: Urban Institute Projections from 1987 National Medical Expediture Survey Tape 18.
Note: These figures do not include nondurable medical goods or charges for telephone consultation.

DISTINGUISHING BETWEEN SHORT- AND LONG-RUN PROBLEMS

Medicare essentially faces two sets of financing problems. The first and more immediate problem is driven by the high costs of health care. The second problem is the demographic issue of the declining contributor-to-beneficiary ratio—the same issue facing Social Security. The first problem essentially explains why Medicare, as opposed to Social Security, is financially unsound at present.

Solutions to these two problems are likely to differ, although they both need to be part of the debate over Medicare's future. To retain solvency in the Part A trust fund for about 10 years and to slow the rate of growth of Part B requires attention to issues concerning the cost of health care, as well as deliberation over who should pay more to support the program. When the demographic issue is joined, a broader range of options will need to be considered, such as the age of eligibility for Medicare.

Although it is currently fashionable to talk about Medicare spending as being "out of control," it is really health spending in general that deserves this criticism. Nonetheless, Medicare's absolute size and rate of growth cause it to stand out from most other domestic programs, and it has naturally become a target in the current debate about how to balance the federal budget. Medicare is one of the fastest growing programs in the federal budget; during the first 25 years of the program, it gobbled up new resources at the rate of nearly 16 percent a year. In 1995, Medicare will total about $181 billion in federal outlays, and costs are projected to rise at an annual rate of about 10 percent in the future (CBO 1995a). In per capita terms, Medicare is projected to expand at about twice the rate of the gross domestic product (GDP), thus consuming a larger share of our national income each year.[11]

These figures help explain why budget proposals by congressional Republicans have included very large reductions in the future growth rate of Medicare as part of their deficit reduction efforts. Consequently, the short-run problems of Medicare actually include two intertwined issues: the policy impetus to reduce the federal deficit and the need to address the imbalance in the Part A trust funds. Despite claims on both sides of the political aisle, these issues are related, but not necessarily identical, and depending upon which prevails, appropriate solutions may differ as well. For instance, the orders of magnitude of changes between Parts A and B of Medicare matter substantially for the Part A trust fund, but do not affect the deficit issue.

Both of the short-run concerns about Medicare have been around for some time. The Part A trust fund has been within 10 years of exhaustion numerous times since 1970 (O'Sullivan 1995). Since 1980, Medicare has been, each year, a major focus of budget reduction efforts. Many of these cutbacks have centered on reducing payments to providers, but some reductions also have affected beneficiaries. Most recently, as part of the 1994 budget reduction efforts, Medicare was cut by $56 billion. Thus far, these cuts have consistently put off the projected exhaustion of the Part A trust fund by cost-cutting efforts, by an increase in the wage base subject to taxation, and by other small revenue increases.

Nonetheless, current projections put the date of trust fund exhaustion at 2002, less than seven years away (Board of Trustees, Federal HI Trust Fund 1995). And even though we have been this close to exhaustion of the trust fund before, the rate of decline in the trust fund's balance is projected to be very rapid, as shown in figure 5.2. In 1995, income to and outflow from the Part A trust fund is essentially the same. But future income growth will average only about 5.5 percent per year, while outflows will average about 8.1 percent (Board of Trustees, Federal HI Trust Fund 1995). Such a discrepancy quickly creates a major financing gap, drawing down the balance and then eroding interest income as well. The actuaries estimate that to meet

Figure 5.2 MEDICARE PART A TRUST FUND BALANCE (in millions)

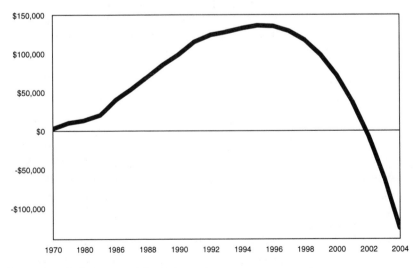

Source: Board of Trustees, Federal Hospital Insurance Trust Fund 1995.

the test of short-run solvency through 2002 (of a balance of one year's expenditure in the trust fund) would require $147 billion in reduced expenditures or higher revenues.

Even strong supporters of the Medicare program thus recognize that substantial changes will be needed both in the short run and in the longer run. And given the current budget climate, most, if not all, of the changes will be in the form of reducing spending.

INCREMENTAL CHANGES AND THE SHORT-RUN PROBLEM

Medicare must begin to slow its rate of growth per capita over time or raise the rate of growth of revenues into the system if it hopes to bring any semblance of stability to the Part A trust fund in the near future. Options considered here are incremental in the sense that they basically leave the system intact and hence could be implemented quickly. But in some cases they may result in substantial savings to the system and will not be treated by many supporters of Medicare as "incremental."

Indeed, particularly if combined with modest revenue increases, it should be possible to use "incremental" changes in Medicare spending to push back the date of exhaustion of the Part A trust fund by at least 10 years. This should be long enough to enable Social Security and Medicare to be viewed in tandem when debating the changes necessary to deal with the long-term demographic problems. Although many observers will argue that it is naive to propose revenue increases at this time, we conclude this section with an assessment of some revenue options.

Provider Payments

One major tool for Medicare is its control over what it pays providers, and indeed, this represents the major source of savings obtained from Medicare in the 1980s.[12] It is both feasible and likely that more of these types of changes will be sought in the near future—at least as interim means for achieving savings before more dramatic restructuring of the program might begin.

There are, however, limits on how much needed savings could come from this source. For example, if providers were paid just enough to keep up with general inflation (the overall CPI), we would be freezing the rate of growth of fees in real terms. Such efforts may be acceptable for a year or two, but it would be very hard to sustain repeated annual cuts or freezes in such payments. At some point, providers of care would revolt and refuse to take Medicare patients. Moreover, even freezes provide limited savings. Payments to physicians under Medicare were "frozen" in the mid-1990s. Nonetheless, the rate of growth of Part B still exceeded 10 percent for that year—both because of some "gaming" of the system and because of an increase in the use of services (Moon 1993).

At present, Medicare's payment levels are below the amount allowed by most private insurers—even those that seek to stress discounts as a means of holding down health care spending (Zuckerman and Verrilli 1995). This likely limits how much further Medicare can go with such activities. The impact of further widening the Medicare/private pay differential could be felt by patients in terms of lower access to care if, for example, doctors decline to accept new Medicare patients. On the other hand, as private plans continue to seek deep discounts and push prices down further, the differential between the two sectors might diminish, thus allowing Medicare to also continue to hold down prices to providers.

The most obvious area to seek savings from lowering Medicare payment levels would seem to be that of inpatient hospital payments, which constitute a large share of overall Medicare spending—about 44 percent in 1995, for example. Indeed, the Congressional Budget Office (1995b) suggests that over a five-year period, a one-year freeze in payment rates to hospitals could save the Medicare program about $6.6 billion. But ironically, projections of future growth suggest that inpatient hospital services are the slowest-growing component of Medicare. And the next largest component, physician services, is the second slowest growing one. Moreover, payment reforms for hospitals and physicians have already generated considerable savings over time, and those areas are on a reasonable footing in terms of basic payment policy. Other areas of Medicare still rely on cost-based reimbursement systems that need to be reformed. In particular, payments for outpatient hospital services and home health care, both rapidly growing areas, need reform and could yield modest savings.

Restrictions on Use of Services

Reductions in spending of the magnitude described previously will also require efforts to rein in the use of new technology and reduce the growth in service use, in addition to provider payment reductions.

One approach would restrict what services are covered or under what circumstances they will be reimbursed. This could either be done by the federal government or by managed-care systems—an option discussed as a structural change later in this chapter. Although such changes would be easier if the whole health care system were reformed—given that Medicare's rapid growth is reflective of problems with the health care system as a whole—reductions in Medicare spending will not and should not be delayed in the absence of such reform.

Medicare can learn some lessons from innovation in the private sector, but as a public program it faces more constraints in terms of accountability and due process, making it difficult to undertake some of these methods. At least five of Medicare's service areas require additional attention: home health services, skilled nursing facility (SNF) care, outpatient hospital services, clinical laboratory services, and durable medical equipment. The first three of these have grown swiftly in recent years, in part because of the changing health care system that is encouraging care to be delivered less intensively as reliance on inpatient hospital care is declining. Thus, some of this growth is certainly desirable. Nonetheless, the expansion of these services has outpaced Medicare's ability to oversee such care. These areas are still largely paid on the basis of costs, and there is almost no control on the necessity of services, thus encouraging rapid growth. Similarly, clinical laboratory services and durable medical equipment are also areas with minimal oversight, and likely result in Medicare paying for unnecessary tests and equipment.

Consider the example of home health services. Costs for such services are reimbursed up to a ceiling, but we do not know, for example, how long each visit lasts, how many separate services are provided at one point in time, or even how many services patients with various characteristics are receiving (Kenney and Moon 1995). The available data suggest that home health aide services provided by proprietary agencies account for much of the explosive growth in this area. New standards, reforms in payment policy, and careful assessment of service provision through profiling of providers and beneficiaries are in order. Specific limits may be needed on particular types of visits or in relation to particular diagnoses. In sum, there is much that Medicare can and should do to improve its oversight of home health care services. These do not have to be accomplished via a capitated mechanism or through private plans. However, improvements will require considerable new administrative effort, and perhaps even an increase in spending on administration.[13]

In fact, many of the innovations in the private sector do not rely upon fixed budgets or capitation. Rather, they apply strict principles for appropriateness of care and are beginning to use sophisticated computer programs for profiling use of services (Ratner 1995). Many of these techniques could be readily adopted by Medicare, with some investment in the necessary tools and training (Etheredge 1995).

On the other hand, Medicare might have difficulty adopting some tools. For example, when a private plan has decided it does not like the way a physician or other provider is delivering care, the plan can simply choose not to contract with that provider any longer. Private plans can also set strict limits on service use, but then grant exceptions in certain cases. They can, in other words, be rather arbitrary in their responses but then move quickly to address problems they see. Medicare is always likely to be much more bound to due process rules and other constraints. This means that Medicare will miss some opportunities to save from inappropriate use of services, but sometimes it will also do better at giving providers the benefit of the doubt. There are both advantages and disadvantages in the flexibility that the private sector can offer.

Increasing the Medicare Premium

One of the most likely approaches for scaling back the Medicare program would be to change the Part B premium that beneficiaries now pay. In 1995, an elderly enrollee is required to pay a premium equal to about 31.5 percent of the costs of Part B, although under current law that share will decline substantially in the future. Raising the Part B premium—or even keeping it a constant percentage—would represent a simple policy change, would raise substantial revenue, and would be consistent with original legislative intent. On the other hand, it would also mean an increasing burden on beneficiaries since premium costs are likely to rise faster than income over time.

Under the original legislation, this premium was set at 50 percent of the costs of physician and related services covered by Part B. After 1966, the growth in the premium far exceeded the growth of Social Security benefits, and it was effectively crowding out other consumption by the elderly. In 1972, the formula was thus decoupled from the costs of Part B and set to rise at the same rate as Social Security benefit payments—that is, it was tied to the consumer price index. Because Medicare costs rose so rapidly over the next eight years, the share of Part B costs covered by the premium fell dramatically to about 25 percent of the overall costs of providing Part B.

The policy change did protect beneficiaries, but more of Medicare's costs were shifted to the federal government. Consequently, as part of the emphasis in the early Reagan years of cutting the federal budget, the growth in the premium was again tied to a share of the costs beginning in 1981. But the share was left at 25 percent, and since then this "temporary" change has been periodically extended. An additional change in 1990 put the exact amounts of the monthly premium in legislation for 1992 through 1995. Although the amount was supposed to represent 25 percent of costs, Part B spending grew more slowly than expected over the period, and hence the percentage has been slowly creeping upward, to its current share of about 31.5 percent. Figure 5.3 depicts the contrast between what premiums would have been if still tied to 50 percent of Part B spending and the actual premium experience. In 1996, the premium is scheduled to again be set at 25 percent, meaning that if there is no policy change, it will actually decline in dollar terms between 1995 and 1996. And after 1999, the 25 percent requirement expires and the premium presumably returns to the growth rate of the Social Security COLA.

How high should the premium be? At 25 percent of Part B, the premium represents only about 10 percent of the overall costs of Med-

Figure 5.3 MEDICARE PART B PREMIUM PER ENROLLEE, HISTORICAL AND AT 50 PERCENT OF INCURRED COSTS

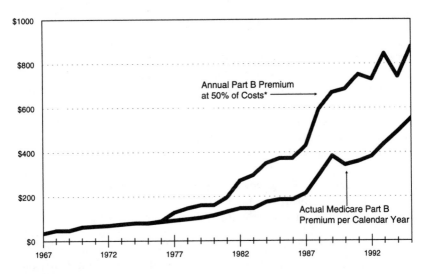

*For year ending June 30.
Source: Board of Trustees, Federal Supplementary Medical Insurance Trust Fund 1995.

icare (Moon 1993). Thus, this premium contribution constitutes a considerably smaller share of total spending as compared to most employer-subsidized plans, which require families to pay about 20 or 25 percent of the costs of their premiums (Sullivan et al. 1992). On the other hand, Medicare benefits are also less comprehensive than those offered to younger families, and many older Americans must pay all or a substantial share of the costs of supplemental Medigap premiums. Since premiums for standard plans tend to average about $800 to $900, Medicare beneficiaries are paying total premiums that are substantially higher than the share of insurance paid by many younger families. Moreover, these premiums constitute about 10 percent of family income for the elderly (see chapter 2). The question of how far to raise these premiums thus is likely to be controversial. Nonetheless, at least retaining the 25 percent share, or increasing it modestly, makes sense as part of a package of changes to meet the future needs of Medicare.[14]

Over time, a variety of proposals have been made to increase premium contributions, usually as part of the annual deficit reduction debates. These can be divided into across-the-board proposals and income-related options. Proposed across-the-board increases are usually quite modest—for example, maintaining premiums near their current level (for example, 30 percent of Part B costs), because an across-the-board increase would have particularly negative consequences on persons with relatively low incomes. But a 30 percent premium requirement will still generate considerable Medicare savings over time. The Congressional Budget Office (1995b) estimated five-year savings of $26.3 billion from this provision.

An increase in the premium to 50 percent would raise the required contribution from individuals to about $1,048 per year (in 1996 dollars). This increase would both raise substantial revenues to cover Medicare costs and pass considerably higher burdens onto beneficiaries—especially those with moderate incomes. Since this would be an increase six times as large as the increase to 30 percent, federal savings would also increase by about that order of magnitude—raising nearly $160 billion over five years. But the increase in liabilities for elderly beneficiaries would also be dramatic. For example, a single person with an income of $15,000—over twice the poverty level— would now devote 7 percent of his or her income just for Part B premiums. And finally, because the Medicaid program usually pays for the premiums of those who are dually enrolled in Medicare and Medicaid or in the QMB program, costs to states would also rise enormously as well.

Income-Related Premium Changes

Although modest increases in premium contributions could likely be absorbed across the board by many Medicare beneficiaries without great difficulty, increasing reliance on this mechanism to "solve" a large portion of the financing problem for Medicare would likely necessitate that an income-related premium be used. A 50 percent premium would represent an inordinate burden on older Americans with moderate incomes. Consequently, to raise even more revenues from premiums, it is tempting to seek income-related increases, as were contained in the Medicare Catastrophic Coverage Act of 1988.[15]

The challenge is to find a politically acceptable change that recognizes both the need for reducing federal outlays on Medicare and the limited ability of many older Americans to take on ever-greater health care burdens. If the limits where income-related burdens begin are set high, they will raise few new revenues. But to obtain substantive increases in revenues means higher premiums on middle-income families, and this may be much less popular politically. Many of the 1994 health reform proposals advocated an income-related premium, suggesting that the fears of a negative reaction similar to that for the Medicare Catastrophic legislation have waned over time and that premium increases are likely in some form in the near future. All of those proposals, however, would have affected only a small number of beneficiaries, since they would not begin to take effect until incomes reached at least $75,000. If more dramatic moves are made to reduce Medicare's spending, the income cutoff for such premiums would likely have to be lowered considerably.

Although opponents of relating the premium to income argue that this approach runs counter to Medicare's basic principles and could undermine the continuing strong public support for Medicare, to some extent we have already moved to an income-related system with the Qualified Medicare Beneficiary (QMB) program, as well as with the dedication of some of the taxation of Social Security benefits that help support the Part A trust fund. In the second case, those tax revenues implicitly operate like an income-related Part A premium. Single persons with incomes above $34,000 and couples with incomes above $44,000 must pay income tax on 85 percent of their Social Security benefits, and part of that tax goes to the Part A trust fund.[16] This "premium" is effectively graduated by the level of Social Security benefits received. The QMB program, on the other hand, provides premium relief only for those with incomes under 120 percent of the poverty guidelines—that is, just under $9,000 in income for a single person in 1995.

The traditional way to conceive of an income-related premium is for one or several increases to be added at the top of the income distribution. But an alternative would be to expand the QMB program and then phase it out, in concert with a general overall increase in the Part B premium.[17] These constitute very different philosophical approaches, in which the expanded QMB approach would concentrate on protecting low-income beneficiaries from increases, rather than distinguishing between moderate- and high-income beneficiaries, which is the focus of the traditional income-related approach. A combination of these two approaches could also be used.

Most of the traditional income-related proposals would have added a new premium on top of the existing Part B premium, usually phased in for individuals or couples above a particular level of income, and reaching a maximum for all persons above a higher income cutoff. For example, the proposal contained in the Clinton health reform bill would have added a new 75 percent premium for single persons with incomes over $105,000 and for couples with incomes over $130,000. This strategy allows the top premium to be much higher than the level feasible under a flat premium increase. In fact, other proposals go so far as to require beneficiaries to pay the full actuarial costs of Part B for those in the top tier.

What is the appropriate point to begin increasing the premium? This is a difficult question to answer and one that will ultimately be quite subjective. Most proponents of an income-related premium advocate that the rise in premiums not begin until people have incomes above at least $75,000 per year. Such premiums would affect very few people and hence would not raise large amounts of revenue. Opponents of income-relating the premium fear that this is just the beginning, however, and that the thresholds would be lowered over time.[18] An additional issue is that of what the premiums should be raised to, which likely depends upon where the threshold levels are set. If the thresholds are very high (say, $60,000 or $75,000 in income for a couple), then it is feasible to raise the share paid by beneficiaries to a higher level than if the thresholds affect those with more moderate incomes.

To illustrate the impact of several different premium proposals, consider two different approaches. The first would income-relate the premiums while retaining the existing QMB program. The second would expand the QMB program to 150 percent of the poverty guidelines and move it to Medicare in an attempt to increase participation.[19] For each of these two options, a wide range of income cutoffs and premium changes is possible. Two income cutoff levels are relevant. The first of these represents the point at which the premium begins to rise with income and we assume that it then rises steadily until reaching the maximum at the second cutoff level. Distinctions are made between singles and couples, so four sets of numbers are actually involved. Table 5.3 indicates how much revenue from the premium would increase under various alternative income-related schemes as compared to the revenue base in current law for 1996— that is, a 25 percent premium. Since our data are limited to persons age 65 and over who are not in institutions, the estimates shown here do not capture the full Medicare beneficiary population and hence should not be thought of as formal cost estimates.[20] Rather, they are interesting for comparison of the relative revenue increases from different combinations of income cutoffs and premium levels.

The highest savings shown in table 5.3 generate over a 50 percent increase in revenues by setting the basic premium at 30 percent and the top premium at 60 percent and beginning the increases in premiums at a relatively low income cutoff. The premium actually begins to rise at $25,000 of income for singles and $30,000 for couples, and reaches 60 percent for incomes of $32,000 and $45,000 for singles and couples, respectively. The lowest savings result from retaining the current 25 percent revenue base and raising it to 50 percent for singles and couples with incomes above $60,000 and $80,000, respectively. In the middle are four options that raise very similar amounts of revenue and illustrate the impact of different variations on revenues raised. Option 7 is consistent with a CBO projection of 5 year savings of $13.9 billion (CBO 1995b).

Several striking conclusions are evident from table 5.3. First, the increase in the bottom tier boosts savings the most. The options in which the bottom tier stays at 25 percent raise the least amount of revenue, even when the top tier is raised to 75 percent. In fact, this impact can be directly compared by looking at the difference between options 5 and 7, in which the only difference is the premium for the bottom tier. Nearly 19 percent more revenue can be raised under option 5 than under option 7. Another finding is that across a certain range, lowering the top tier income cutoff does not increase savings by much. Compare for example, options 2 and 4. This suggests that setting a relatively high income cutoff for political purposes may not reduce savings as much as one might assume. But in the more moderate income range (i.e., options 1 and 3), changes do make a difference.

Finally, increasing the QMB protection (and assuming a higher participation rate and full federal funding) substantially reduces the savings from the income-related premium proposals shown here. For

Table 5.3 ESTIMATED REVENUE INCREASES AS SHARE OF CURRENT PART B PREMIUM FROM INCOME-RELATED OPTIONS, 1996

	Option			Premium Increase as Share of Current Law Premium Revenues Assuming:	
	Premium Levels as Percentage of Part B Costs	Income Phase-in for Singles/Couples ($)	Income Where Top Rate Fully Phased-in (Singles/Couples) ($)	Continuation of Existing QMB Program (%)[a]	Expanded QMB Program (%)[b]
1	30% & 60%	25,000/30,000	32,000/45,000	154.8	136.1
2	30% & 75%	60,000/75,000	80,000/100,000	129.3	110.6
3	30% & 60%	60,000/75,000	80,000/100,000	126.1	107.5
4	30% & 75%	90,000/105,000	115,000/130,000	124.4	105.7
5	30% & 50%	50,000/65,000	60,000/80,000	126.2	107.5
6	25% & 75%	60,000/75,000	80,000/100,000	110.4	94.8
7	25% & 50%	50,000/65,000	60,000/80,000	107.8	92.2

Source: Authors' estimates using March 1993 Current Population Survey.
a. Includes 41 percent of those with incomes below 120 percent of poverty guidelines, as well as state share of Qualified Medicare Beneficiaries (QMB).
b. Includes 65 percent of those with incomes below 150 percent of poverty guidelines and assumes no state contributions.

example, if one of the intermediate options were chosen (options 2 through 5 in table 5.3), revenues would rise by only about 5 to 10 percent. If a phaseout of the QMB program were also introduced for those with incomes above 120 or 150 percent of poverty, the costs of expanding the QMB program could be even higher. On the other hand, a large share of this increased cost comes from relieving states of the costs of QMB. For example, revenue as a share of current spending under option 2 would decline to about 136 percent (rather than 110.6 percent) if states were still required to contribute for QMB.

It is interesting to compare how much premiums would have to rise across the board to produce revenue increases comparable to those generated by some of the income-related options in table 5.3. Table 5.4 offers two different versions of a flat premium, depending upon what would happen to QMB protection. The first set of numbers retains the QMB program as though it kept the 120 percent QMB benefit and the same participation. The second set of numbers assumes an increase in the level of incomes protected by the QMB program to 150 percent of poverty and a 65 percent participation rate funded fully by the federal government. The annual flat premiums would have to be raised even further under the QMB expansion assumption to make up for revenues lost by reducing the number of people who must pay the flat premium and the loss of state revenues. These flat premium increases can be compared with current law projections of $524.

Changing Cost Sharing

When Medicare began in 1966, the deductibles for Part A and Part B were set at nearly the same level: $40 and $50, respectively. But over time the Part A deductible has grown substantially to $716 in 1995,

Table 5.4 FLAT PREMIUM INCREASES NECESSARY TO RAISE REVENUES COMPARABLE TO INCOME-RELATED OPTIONS

Revenue Increase from Income-Related Options (%)[a]	Annual Premium Increase (in 1996 dollars) Necessary when QMB Protection Set at:	
	120% of Poverty	150% or Poverty
154.8	287	340
144.1	231	315
129.3	154	233
107.8	41	113

Source: Authors' simulations using 1993 Current Population Survey, U.S. Bureau of the Census.
a. As defined in table 5.3.

compared to just $100 for Part B. Coinsurance is assessed on all physician services and on some hospital and skilled nursing facility days, but not on home health benefits or laboratory services. This combination of deductibles and coinsurance for Medicare represents an ad hoc collection of payments with little defensible justification as points of control for the use of health care services. Thus, it makes sense to reshape this cost sharing either in a budget-neutral way or to achieve some net savings.

The goal of cost sharing is to provide cost awareness and thus give beneficiaries incentives to carefully use services. But the importance of these incentives varies by type of health care service. For example, most analysts believe that hospital deductibles and coinsurance do little to discourage use of such services. Patients rarely make the decision to check into a hospital on their own. Moreover, there are other constraints on use of hospital care, such as preadmission screening, that serve to limit inappropriate use. And Medicare gives hospitals strong incentives to release their patients as early as possible, reducing the justification for coinsurance on the days of very long stays. Consequently, hospital cost sharing—which is particularly high under Medicare—could be reduced or eliminated with no expected increase in the use of services. Table 5.5 illustrates the per capita

Table 5.5 NET REDUCTIONS IN PER CAPITA OUT-OF-POCKET LIABILITIES FROM CHANGES IN HOSPITAL DEDUCTIBLES AND COINSURANCE, 1994

	Net Reductions in Liability from:		
Characteristic	Eliminating All Coinsurance and Deductibles ($)	Replacing Existing Cost Sharing with One $250 Deductible ($)	Replacing Existing Cost Sharing with One $500 Deductible ($)
Poverty Status:			
Under 100%	$163	$104	$44
100–125%	127	68	7
125–200%	116	63	9
200–400%	257	209	160
Over 400%	172	129	87
Age:			
65–69	89	48	6
70–74	145	100	55
75–79	181	125	70
80–84	405	344	281
85 +	428	352	276
All Elderly	186	136	85

Source: Authors' simulations using National Medical Expenditure Survey.

costs of such a reduction and illustrates how the reduction would be distributed across income and age groups. As expected, the oldest beneficiaries would be likely to benefit the most.[21] Low-income beneficiaries are already somewhat protected by the QMB program, which is why those with incomes under 100 percent of poverty benefit to a lesser degree. In 1995, however, hospital cost sharing will save the federal government about $7.8 billion by shifting costs onto beneficiaries and/or employers who help pay a share of retirees' health insurance. Eliminating or reducing this cost sharing would thus be expensive (Board of Trustees, Federal HI Trust Fund 1995).

Another candidate for reductions in cost sharing is the coinsurance on skilled nursing facility (SNF) services. When the program was established in 1965, the coinsurance was set at one-eighth the hospital deductible. But over time, hospital costs have risen faster than costs of SNF care, raising this coinsurance to an unreasonably high level. This effectively restricts the number of days of SNF care available to beneficiaries to about 20 days, rather than the 100 days that are in the legislation. This cost sharing would also be expensive to eliminate, however, since it is estimated that it will bring in $1.7 billion to Medicare in 1995 (Board of Trustees, Federal HI Trust Fund 1995), but it could be reworked to add cost sharing in the early days of a stay in return for a lower level of coinsurance overall.

Finally, totally missing from Medicare is any upper-bound limit on cost-sharing liabilities. Beneficiaries with complicated illnesses (and no Medigap protection) can end up owing tens of thousands of dollars in Medicare cost sharing. Thus, adding stop-loss protection—that is, the guarantee that above a certain threshold, the individual should not have to continue to pay out-of-pocket for Medicare-covered services—would be a valuable addition to Medicare. But stop-loss protection for this age group would be very expensive to provide. In the absence of stop loss, care should be taken not to overextend other cost-sharing increases.

In Medicare, the most likely areas for expanding cost sharing are in adding coinsurance for home health services and raising the level of the Part B deductible. More and more enrollees exceed the Part B deductible each year since it has not kept up with Part B spending. It could be raised to $250 or $300 per year and still be comparable to or lower than that found in many private insurance plans. Table 5.6 shows the distributional impact of the liabilities from such an increase. In general, these burdens are relatively evenly distributed across age and income groups, since many of the elderly would be affected by this change.

Table 5.6 NET INCREASES IN PER CAPITA OUT-OF-POCKET LIABILITIES FOR
ELDERLY BENEFICIARIES FROM PART B DEDUCTIBLE AND HOME
HEALTH COINSURANCE CHANGES, 1994

	Net New Liabilities from:		
	Raising Part B Deductible to:		Adding 20% Home Health
Characteristic	$250 ($)	$300 ($)	Coinsurance ($)
Poverty Status:			
Under 100%	42	55	92
100–125%	63	84	99
125–200%	73	96	105
200–400%	77	102	30
Over 400%	83	109	54
Age:			
65–69	69	91	35
70–74	73	97	52
75–79	76	101	56
80–84	76	100	62
85+	68	90	241
All Elderly	72	95	64

Source: Authors' simulations using NMES.

The reintroduction of coinsurance for home health services might
help to slow the growth in this part of the Medicare program. When
the original coinsurance requirement for home health was eliminated
in 1972, use of that benefit grew rapidly, particularly on the Part A
side of Medicare (Kenney 1990). A first look at the distributional
impact of a 20 percent coinsurance (see table 5.6) suggests that although more unevenly distributed than raising the deductible, the
impact is still relatively small. However, because people with home
health visits tend to receive them for an extended period of time,
coinsurance can mount up very quickly for these services. For example, a 20 percent coinsurance would raise the out-of-pocket burdens
on the average home health recipient by over $1,100 if instituted in
1995 (see table 5.7). In addition, this home health coinsurance would
fall particularly heavily on the old and the frail, who also tend to have
lower incomes. While private supplemental insurance would moderate this impact, approximately 200,000 elderly beneficiaries who have
no protection other than Medicare would be directly affected by this
coinsurance (Moon 1995).

A better approach would be to shift home health to Part B, where
it would be subject to the premium, and limit any copayment to a

Table 5.7 AVERAGE INCREASE IN MEDICARE LIABILITIES FOR HOME HEALTH
USERS, 1994

	20% Home Health Coinsurance
Age:	
65 to 69	$1,242
70 to 74	1,294
75 to 79	795
80 to 84	760
85 +	1,410
Poverty Status:	
<100%	$ 976
100 to 124%	1,198
125 to 199%	1,515
200 to 399%	634
400% +	1,439
Total Out-of-Pocket:	
<$300	$1,209
$300 to $999	670
$1000 to $4999	867
$5000 +	1,905
Total	$1,109

Source: Authors' simulations using National Medical Expenditure Survey.

nominal amount of perhaps 5 percent of costs, or $5 per visit, for example. Alternatively, any copayment could be limited to services received after a period of time or only for home health aide services.[22] Moreover, controls on use of services might be better directed at the supply of such care either through improved guidelines or actual limits on numbers of services.

Overall restructuring of Medicare cost sharing could improve the Medicare program by shifting cost sharing to those areas where the incentives might be more effective. This could be done in a relatively budget-neutral way with increases in some areas offsetting changes in others, and by simplifying the program and making it more consistent with insurance on the under-65 population. A problem arises, however, because such changes would raise federal outlays under Part A while reducing them under Part B. Unless some means of redressing this imbalance can be found, such a change would exacerbate the Part A trust fund outlook. (This issue is discussed in more detail later in this chapter.)

In addition, the QMB program could be expanded to improve protection of the low-income population from cost sharing in a manner analogous to the premium changes already described. If cost-sharing improvements overall become too expensive to provide—for example, in the case of stop-loss protections—one way to offer at least partial relief would be to expand the QMB program. At least in theory, the QMB program now provides stop-loss for those with the lowest incomes. And although participation is low (Neumann et al. 1994), about 10 to 12 percent of Medicare enrollees now potentially have this protection. It has likely helped an additional 4 to 5 percent of the elderly population hold down out-of-pocket expenses. Thus, one less-expensive way to provide some protection for the most vulnerable beneficiaries would be to expand the QMB program, say, to 150 percent of the poverty level and seek ways to increase participation in it.

Other Incremental Changes

In addition to the various options for reducing spending just described, some adjustments in the program make sense that would not necessarily reduce federal spending overall but could streamline Medicare and improve the status of the Part A trust fund. These options also should be considered if the goal is to protect Medicare and not just to reduce the federal budget deficit.

As Medicare changes over time, it makes little sense to maintain two separate parts to the program. Parts A and B were created as a last-minute compromise in the original legislation (Moon 1993). But over time, they have become closely linked, and changes in Part A affect Part B and vice versa. For example, the introduction of the prospective payment system for hospitals likely moved costs from A to B by speeding up the shift of many procedures out of inpatient hospital care to outpatient services (which are covered under Part B). Because these two halves of Medicare operate differently and have different financing streams, a number of issues must be resolved before they can be combined. Nonetheless, Parts A and B could be merged and financing issues addressed in toto.

If that is deemed too large a change in the short run, one alteration that would be beneficial to the Part A trust fund would be to shift home health services out of Part A and into Part B. There is historical precedent for such a change, since in the early days of the program, a substantial share of home health was funneled through Part B. And as an ambulatory service, it also makes logical sense to move it out of Part A, which otherwise covers inpatient hospital and skilled nursing care—both institutionally based services.

Shifting home health from Part A to Part B would reduce the Part A trust fund outflow substantially—by about $110 billion from 1996 to 2000 (CBO 1995a)—simply because home health care would no longer be paid out of Part A. It would save the overall Medicare program substantial resources as well, because part of the costs of home health would now be borne by beneficiaries through the premium they are required to pay for that part of Medicare. Shifting home health into Part B would have raised the monthly premium by about $10 per month in 1996 (assuming the premium is 25 percent of costs as scheduled under current law). If the premium is increased to 30 percent, the premium would go up about $144 per year for home health services, in addition to the $105 annual rise from the increased premium share from 25 to 30 percent). This burden would be evenly spread across most beneficiaries, except for those at the bottom of the distribution who would have QMB protection.

Finally, Medicare now cross-subsidizes a number of worthy activities including graduate medical education and support for hospitals serving particularly vulnerable populations. But if some or all of Medicare shifts to private plans over time, a phasing down of these subsidies will implicitly occur. And the portion that remains Medicare fee-for-service will be at a disadvantage if it is still required to be the mechanism for such subsidies. Thus, a good case can be made to "clean up" the Medicare program so that dedicated revenues are used only to finance care for the elderly and disabled and not to achieve other worthy goals. For example, eliminating direct payments to medical education and substantially reducing payments for indirect costs of hospital teaching programs could save over $20 billion from 1996 to 2000 (CBO 1995b). A gradual elimination of disproportionate-share payments for hospitals serving high numbers of Medicare and Medicaid patients would save about $13.4 billion over the same period. The danger is that these activities—especially protection of care for low-income persons—will not be shifted elsewhere but simply will be lost in the process. Again, part of the issue is whether changes in Medicare will be sought to improve the program's stability or to make a major contribution to reducing the federal deficit. The changes described in this section would largely address the former issue rather than the latter.

Revenue Issues

Although a discussion of increased revenues to support Medicare more likely belongs in an analysis of what to do about Medicare after 2010 when the demographic issues become predominant, some smaller-scale revenue increases might be in order, particularly to protect the Part A trust fund. These revenue changes might not even result in actual increases in aggregate taxes but, rather, in a shift from the Social Security OASI trust fund revenues in order to put the two trust funds on more of an equal footing.[23] For example, the share of the FICA tax of 7.65 percent that goes to Medicare could be raised. Alternatively, more of the taxation of Social Security benefits—or an expansion of that taxation—could be directed to Medicare's Part A trust fund.

A small increase in the payroll tax share devoted to Medicare could raise substantially the revenue base for the program. For example, if the 1.45 percent share were increased just to 1.5 percent, revenues in fiscal year 1996 would rise by about $3.7 billion.[24] Over the years, these shares have often been shifted back and forth. Indeed, a 1973 amendment to the Social Security Act allocated Medicare's portion as 1.5 percent, to begin in 1986 (U.S. Social Security Administration 1988). Later amendments rolled the share back to 1.45 percent. Thus, an increase in Medicare's FICA share to 1.5 or 1.6 percent could be used to help defray the amount needed to resolve Part A's short-run problems.

Alternatively (or in addition to the preceding change), Medicare could receive additional funds from the taxation of Social Security benefits. As noted, this revenue operates essentially like an income-related premium for Part A. Every dollar paid by higher-income beneficiaries goes to help fund benefits to Medicare beneficiaries. Effectively, this is a way to make the Medicare program more progressive as well, without generating new administrative structures to do so. The Treasury Department estimates that this provision will add $15 billion to the Medicare trust fund over the next 5 years, and $48.5 billion between 1995 and 2005. The share of revenues directed to Part A, however, represents only part of what is raised through taxation of Social Security benefits. The bottom tier (i.e., taxation of 50 percent of benefits beginning at a lower threshold) goes to the Social Security trust funds. Some of that could be shifted to Medicare. Alternatively, lowering the threshold for applying the 85 percent tax (as discussed in chapter 4) could add even more revenues to the Part A trust fund while leaving the portion for Social Security intact.

TAXING THE VALUE OF MEDICARE BENEFITS

An alternative to raising premiums would be to treat Medicare benefits—all or in part—as income and subject to the federal personal income tax. If, for example, half of the average value of benefits were added to the incomes of the elderly and disabled, these benefits would be subject to tax rates that would vary according to other income received, naturally resulting in a progressive tax on Medicare benefits. This is analogous to taxing Social Security, but is more complicated because Medicare benefits are received "in-kind" and are not traditionally viewed as income by the beneficiaries.

To treat Medicare benefits as income would not only raise revenue to help fund the current program (or expansions in Medicare), but it would also make beneficiaries more acutely aware of the "value" of Medicare benefits and their rate of growth over time. If a portion of benefits were taxed, but only for those whose incomes are above some threshold, mostly high-income beneficiaries would be affected.[25] This could satisfy many who now advocate providing universal benefits to elderly and disabled persons regardless of their economic circumstances, while not removing them from eligibility.

This option represents a substantial change in policy, and would add considerably to the complexity of the program while raising relatively small amounts for Medicare. Critics of this approach also argue that it is unfair to tax some in-kind benefits and not others. Consistency would imply that we should tax health benefits provided by employers to their workers as well—also a very controversial policy.

In a recent analysis of this type of approach, the Congressional Budget Office (1994d) examined taxation of entitlements as an alternative to means-testing. They concluded that taxation would be considerably easier to administer than means-testing, but would affect more individuals in a less-progressive way. They also pointed out, however, that progressivity could be increased—for example, by exempting some entitlements or establishing a threshold of income before taxation begins (similar to what now happens under Social Security). If all entitlements were subject to taxation, 60 percent of the elderly would be affected, and benefits would effectively fall by about 11 percent.

PROSPECTS FOR MAJOR RESTRUCTURING OF MEDICARE

The terms of the debate over Medicare's future are changing dramatically. The focus has shifted from the 1994 discussion of minor expansions in some areas and substantial savings in others to a simple

emphasis in 1995 on large reductions in spending on Medicare beginning immediately. The large numbers of dollars scheduled to be saved
from Medicare have encouraged some legislators to consider radical
restructuring of the program. Sometimes billed as painless (Wines
1995), sometimes as simply necessary, proposals for restructuring
have moved from the highly speculative and unlikely to being viewed
as more respectable. However, with one exception noted in this section, there is little evidence to indicate that enormous savings are
readily available, particularly in the short run.

Restructuring proposals deserve attention, not because they offer
magic bullets but, rather, because this is the direction that mainstream
medical care is headed and because offering choices to beneficiaries
may represent an improvement in the program. Since the health care
delivery system in the United States seems to be moving rapidly toward some form of managed care, it will be increasingly difficult—
and likely undesirable—to ignore this area. And Medicare already has
a managed-care option that needs improvement regardless of any expansions. Thus, the issue essentially is how far along a continuum
toward managed care or other decentralized options we wish to go.
Medicare needs to adopt at least some of the strategies used by managed care or find ways to improve its current optional HMO program.
But great care is needed here, because major problems are associated
with the laudable goal of expanding choice.

Two types of major restructuring of Medicare are beginning to receive serious attention: options for turning Medicare into a voucher
program and changing the way that care is delivered to rely on some
form of managed care. Although these two elements could be combined, each implies important changes for Medicare that have different implications. Moreover, it is possible to have one without the other.
For example, Medicare beneficiaries could simply be given vouchers
to purchase whatever type of insurance they wish—subject to insurers
meeting certain standards. This would give beneficiaries the option
of buying into a health maintenance organization (HMO), some looser
form of managed care, or remaining in a traditional indemnity type
plan. But managed-care options could also be offered to elderly and
disabled persons, by which they could enroll in HMOs or similar
plans but the plans would be certified by Medicare and overseen more
directly—as with the current optional HMO program.

As described in the paragraphs following, the philosophy behind
these two approaches and their mechanisms for saving costs are actually quite different. It is important to consider each of these approaches separately. However, they do share a common important bar-

rier to developing viable options for their expansion—the issue of risk selection and choice, as discussed in the subsection following.

Balancing Choice and Risk

One of the appealing aspects of restructuring from a beneficiary's perspective is likely to be the opportunity to choose among a variety of plans both in terms of the structure of the plan (i.e., fee for service versus health maintenance organizations) and also in terms of services covered. Those who wish to pay higher premiums and lower cost sharing might be accommodated, for example. Some plans might emphasize long-term care or mental health benefits. Others might exclude such benefits as a means of lowering costs. The problem is that allowing choice concerning services covered is inevitably an invitation to plans to package services so as to attract only healthy beneficiaries. And without adequate adjustments for payments to plans based on differences in risk, sicker beneficiaries would be severely disadvantaged. Balancing between desirable choices and undesirable risk selection poses difficult challenges for Medicare.

An essential aspect of any proposal allowing people to choose optional plans is that it set an appropriate overall payment level and then adjust for differences in risk. But this is easier said than done. We do not yet have the knowledge to establish a risk adjustment factor that ensures that 75-year-olds in poor health are as attractive to insurers as healthy 85-year-olds. The current method of paying managed-care plans for Medicare patients is seriously flawed in terms of risk adjustments. A recent study found that the actual cost of serving Medicare beneficiaries who opt for HMO enrollment is 5.7 percent more than Medicare would have paid for these same beneficiaries had they been covered under fee-for-service Medicare coverage. Instead of saving Medicare money, the program loses almost 6 percent for every Medicare managed-care enrollee (Brown et al. 1993).

Given the extreme variability in health outlays among beneficiaries, there is great leeway for plans to select relatively healthier beneficiaries for whom capitated rates exceed true costs. If optional plans succeed in attracting and retaining relatively healthier Medicare beneficiaries—for which they have very strong incentives—Medicare will overpay for those beneficiaries in these optional plans while paying the full cost of the sickest Medicare beneficiaries who remain in a traditional Medicare option (assuming that is the way the program is structured).

Most restructuring plans under discussion would encourage development of optional private plans, often but not always featuring managed care, while keeping the standard Medicare approach as an option. If sufficient protections to guard against risk selection are not in place, there is a danger of creating a fallback Medicare program dominated by high-risk individuals—that is, persons with both low or moderate incomes and health problems that make them unattractive to insurers. In this case, the costs of the Medicare fee-for-service program will skyrocket, not because of its inefficiencies but because of its risk profile of beneficiaries who remain in that part of the program. But this may not mean good news for private plans that participate in Medicare. Indeed, if this fallback portion of Medicare contains mainly very sick, low-income enrollees, it may become more difficult over time to continue raising their premiums and cost sharing. Instead, saving costs may have to come out of payments to private providers.

Alternatively, if out-of-pocket costs are pushed up substantially, many of these high-risk beneficiaries could move out of fee-for-service Medicare and into managed-care plans that are priced low enough to be affordable. These could be of lower quality, but at a minimum would likely be more restrictive than other, higher-priced plans. If the distinction begins to occur between high- and low-priced plans, Medicare may end up with a strongly divided program in which the goal of universal access to a defined benefit is lost.

Vouchers

Advocates of a private approach to financing health care for Medicare enrollees argue for a system of vouchers in which eligible persons would be allowed to choose their own health care plan from among an array of private options. For example, individuals might be able to opt for larger deductibles or coinsurance in return for coverage of other services such as prescription drugs or long-term care. Advocates of medical savings accounts, for example, would argue that such an option should be available to Medicare beneficiaries.[26] In addition, since many Medicare enrollees now choose to supplement Medicare with private insurance, this approach would allow beneficiaries to combine the voucher with their own funds and buy one comprehensive plan. No longer would they have to worry about coordinating coverage between Medicare and their private supplemental plan. Moreover, persons with employer-provided supplemental coverage could remain in the same health care plans they had as employees.

Competition among plans to attract enrollees might help to lower prices, but it also seems likely that there also would be considerable nonprice competition in the marketing strategies of various plans.[27] Moreover, there is nothing about competition itself that guarantees lower prices. The only certain way for Medicare to reduce costs under a voucher scheme would be to fix the payment level and its rate of growth over time. This could ensure substantial savings by effectively shifting Medicare into a defined contribution plan. Benefits would no longer be guaranteed; rather, beneficiaries would simply receive a fixed dollar amount each year to put toward the costs of insurance.

To the government, this option would have the appeal of enabling a predictable rate of growth in the program. For example, the federal government could set the vouchers to grow at the same rate as GDP or some other factor. But most important, such options are usually developed to achieve major cost savings. The "price" of offering choice to enrollees might be a voucher set at 90 or 95 percent of the current level of government spending per enrollee. And even more important, by placing a cap on the rate of growth of the benefit, vouchers effectively shift the risk to the private insurer and/or to the enrollee.

Figures vary on how much of a reduction in growth in the program would be sought from the vouchers. The $270 billion savings target in the budget resolution for 1996 through 2002 would require essentially a 40 percent reduction in the growth rate of per capita Medicare spending, which is projected to grow at about 8.4 percent per year. It has sometimes been suggested that vouchers could bear all this reduction—a very ambitious goal for any single cost-containment mechanism and likely not a very realistic one.

If a plan is not successful in holding down costs and Medicare's contribution is fixed, the most likely response is to raise the supplemental contribution required of enrollees. This is effectively an indirect premium increase on beneficiaries. Advocates of vouchers argue that consumer opposition to paying higher prices would force insurers to hold down costs, and that facing higher costs is thus a good thing and not a problem. Opponents claim that both consumers and insurers would lack the clout to achieve such cost controls.

How successful is the private sector likely to be in holding down costs as compared to the current Medicare program? First, private insurers will almost surely have higher administrative overhead costs than does Medicare. Insurers will need to advertise and promote their plans. They will face a smaller risk pool, which may require them to make more conservative decisions regarding reserves and other protections against losses over time. These plans expect to return a profit to shareholders. All of these factors cumulate and work against private companies performing better than Medicare. At least in the Medicare program, the government's track record at efficiently providing services is quite good, with overhead two to three times less than that in the private market (CRS 1989).

On the other side of the ledger are the possibilities that private insurers may be able to develop new cost-containment schemes that will be more effective. They may be able to bargain for good prices and adapt to changing circumstances more readily than the public sector can. But as noted, Medicare's payment levels are already at the low end of the scale. Finally, by combining coverage of those services that Medicare now covers with other medical care such as preventive services, drugs, and long-term care, the private sector may be able to find better ways to package and deliver care. Such efforts may prove to be popular even if they do not result in lower costs of care.

Regulation would be needed to require insurers to take all comers and to guard against problems of adverse selection whereby one plan may be able to compete by choosing carefully what persons to cover. First, the program is most likely to be problematic if it is voluntary. Further, adverse selection is more likely if Medicare enrollees are free to supplement their vouchers to enhance coverage; insurers may find that those with the most to spend on certain types of supplemental coverage may be the best risks. For example, covering the "extras" such as private rooms and specialized nursing care may appeal to enrollees who are relatively healthy and well-off compared to enrollees attracted to a supplemental package that mainly offers coverage of prescription drugs or those who can only afford the bare minimum package.

The most serious potential problem with vouchers is that the market would begin to divide beneficiaries in ways that put the most vulnerable beneficiaries—those in low health and with modest incomes—at particular risk. If vouchers result in high-cost, cadillac plans or other types of specialized plans like medical savings accounts that skim off the healthier, wealthier beneficiaries, many Medicare enrollees who now have reasonable coverage for acute-care costs, but who are the less-desirable risks, would face much higher costs due to the market segmentation. A two-tier system of care could result in which modest-income families are forced to choose less-desirable plans.

On balance, vouchers offer less in the way of guarantees for continued protection under Medicare. They are most appealing as a way to substantially cut the federal government's contributions to the plan indirectly through erosion of the comprehensiveness of coverage that the private-sector offers rather than as stated policy. The problems of making tough choices and the financial risks would be borne by beneficiaries. Further, the federal government's role in influencing the course of our health care system would be substantially diminished. For some, this is a major positive advantage of such reforms. But the history of Medicare is one in which the public sector has often played a positive role as well, first insuring those largely rejected by the private sector and then leading the way in many cost-containment efforts (Moon 1993). Most troubling, however, is the likelihood that the principle of offering a universal benefit would be seriously undermined.

Managed-Care Options

Rather than creating vouchers that effectively put enrollees at risk, Medicare could move to a system of requiring managed-care arrangements, but with the program still operated and overseen by the federal government, so that the government could continue to share some of the risks. Enrollees could be encouraged or required to operate within an HMO, an independent practice association (IPA), a preferred provider organization (PPO), or some other similar entity paid to offer health care on a per capita basis. All of these organizations seek to control costs by managing the overall level of care that the patient receives, moving away from a system that pays on a per service basis where the more you use, the more the provider makes.

In a well-managed, high-quality capitated system, the individual can receive much better continuity of care. Patient records and information can readily be shared within the organization and services will be better coordinated. Physicians have no incentive to prescribe unnecessary tests or procedures, since that only adds to the costs of care. On the other hand, they also need to perform good diagnostic and preventive services to reduce use of the big-ticket items such as hospitalization. Moreover, if Medicare performs its role as a careful overseer, any propensity to skimp on care can be reduced as well. And in such a system, payments could be made on the basis of the experience of the best providers, rather than locking into some fixed rate of growth.

It is important to look closely at the ways that managed care seeks to hold down costs of care, and to examine those in the context of Medicare and its beneficiaries. As noted above, competition itself does not engender lower costs; rather, competition presumably spurs on plans to seek new and better ways to hold down costs so as to be competitive. The presumption is that this will occur through more aggressive management of the delivery of care. The private sector has been seeking ways to hold down health care spending particularly as compared to traditional indemnity insurance plans by relying essentially on four separate types of tools:

- Lower administrative costs, in part by consciously streamlining management and by having less paperwork since patients are not billed for each service, for example;
- Paying doctors and other providers of care less by engaging in tough negotiations for discounts in exchange for promises of high volume;
- Directly managing care of patients—for example, by setting strict rules on hospital lengths of stays, by offering financial incentives and penalties to control use of tests and referrals to specialists, and by requiring that patients use network providers or pay a large copay if they go outside the system; and
- Carefully marketing products so as to attract good risks—that is, people who are less likely to be high users of health care services.

Will these strategies work well for the Medicare population? If so, it might be possible to obtain large savings by encouraging people not to move into managed care. But, for several of these categories, Medicare may not show the same results as when private employers move their workers from generous indemnity plans into managed care. Special circumstances for Medicare need to be taken into account. And even more important, advocates of privatization of Medicare presume that growth rates can be lowered year after year, so we need to consider whether these savings are sustainable over a long period of time.

Administrative savings may prove problematic as a source of savings for Medicare. First, Medicare's administrative costs are low— ranging from 2 to 4 percent of program outlays—compared to what most managed-care plans achieve. Moreover, if private plans compete for Medicare business, the marketing and advertising costs will be substantial. Start-up costs for new entrants into this market and even for those adding Medicare to existing covered populations may be high as well. For example, who will pay for the reserves necessary to ensure that private plans are on sound financial footing? Adding 5–10 million new insured lives in the private market will pose major capitalization needs. These new plans thus are not likely to save much compared to administrative advantages that accrue to traditional Medicare, particularly in the early years.

Similarly, many managed-care plans have been very attractive to private employers because of the discounts employers receive from providers of care. Rates of payments to hospitals, doctors, and other providers for traditional private indemnity plans are quite high, so discounts can immediately result in lower premiums. Medicare, however, has already obtained discounts in the form of administered prices that are usually well below what private insurers pay, and even below what some managed-care plans now pay (Zuckerman and Verrilli 1995). Thus, in many areas of the country it will be difficult for private plans to drive a harder bargain than Medicare already has. Medicare may already be achieving advantages similar to PPOs whose main sources of savings are from discounts. The likely exception is in areas where managed-care plans essentially are wringing out excess capacity by forcing providers to bid against each other. Some of these very deep discounts likely cannot be sustained over time, and it is not clear whether it is reasonable to expect Medicare to help drive inefficient providers out of the market.

One area where managed care may be able to improve upon Medicare is in truly *managing* services received by patients. Private plans not only can provide closer oversight, but they can be more arbitrary and prescriptive than a national, public program like Medicare. This means that particularly in some areas like home health service use and hospital outpatient services, private plans could provide more controls on service use than Medicare does currently. And although Medicare could certainly exert more control under its present structure, private plans may ultimately be better able to deal with providers who abuse the system by ordering too many tests or even defrauding the government. Private plans can simply exclude problematic providers or place restrictions on their behavior in ways that Medicare would not likely be able to. Nevertheless, it is important to keep a caveat in mind in this regard. Even though Medicare can be limited by the requirements for due process and other legal restrictions, these restraints are not all bad. They help to guarantee access to all patients and providers to the system, and it is important not to give up all such protections in the enthusiasm over managing care.

In addition, older and disabled beneficiaries represent a unique patient type, and many managed care firms have not been anxious to move into this market. It is not the case that one size necessarily fits all; thus, firms that successfully manage care for younger persons may not find it easy to do well in this market. Older patients with multiple health care problems may need to see a specialist regularly, for example, when many managed-care plans seek to limit such contacts as much as possible. Such activities might be less cost-effective for the

Medicare population, and other arrangements might be needed—such as agreements with specialists to be primary care gatekeepers, for example. It will take time for new entrants into this market to develop the expertise to deal effectively with this population.

Managed-care systems mainly save on the costs of care by reducing use. This may reduce unnecessary care, but can also cut into important services as well. Consequently, such organizations often place an important burden on consumers to be aggressive advocates for their own care. The barriers to care that HMOs and others establish to discourage overuse may be intimidating, particularly for the very old or frail. It may be easier to establish barriers to use of services than to carefully manage care on a case-by-case basis. Further, the restrictions on choice implicit in such a system are viewed negatively by many.

Finally, holding down costs by selecting only healthy enrollees is the major problem facing these types of plans, as already described. Saving costs through this strategy is good for specific plans but not good for Medicare as the financially responsible entity.

The promise of managed care and the pressures that will arise over time as the rest of the health care system moves in this direction underscore how crucial is the effort to improve Medicare's managed care. But will such a shift lower the rate of growth sufficiently to achieve the stringent limits that some have in mind for the program? Or will stronger limits that effectively place both the insurer and the beneficiary at risk be required to meet those goals? This is one of the major challenges likely to face Medicare for the foreseeable future.

CHANGES IN ELIGIBILITY

A longer-run strategy for Medicare may be to reduce the number of persons eligible for the program, primarily by using age or income limits. These options become more appealing over the long term, when the numbers of Medicare beneficiaries will rise substantially as a result of the aging of the baby boomers.

Changing Age of Eligibility

The initial age of eligibility for Medicare could be raised. As with Social Security, one of the justifications for such a change—aside from the primary one of saving the system money—is that as the life expectancy of the population has moved upward, the age for receiving benefits should also increase.[28] Since Medicare was introduced in 1966, the life expectancy for persons aged 65 has grown by a little over two years (Census Bureau 1993a), meaning that they now receive Medicare benefits for a greater share of their lifetimes. Thus, increasing the age of eligibility could bring this proportion back to the level anticipated in 1965. In fact, this approach has already been adopted for retirement benefits under Social Security—albeit phased in over a long period. The Social Security Amendments of 1983 established a schedule by which the age of eligibility for full Social Security cash benefits would increase over time from age 65 to age 67 by the year 2022.

For Medicare, the transition would likely need to be somewhat more rapid than the changes established for Social Security in the 1983 amendments, since the financial crisis for the Part A trust funds will come sooner than the trust fund problems for Social Security. For example, age of eligibility could be increased by two months every year until the age of eligibility reached 68. This would reduce the number of eligible elderly people by about 15 percent, although some of those persons would undoubtedly qualify as disabled and hence would still be eligible for Medicare. Alternatively, the phase-in could begin more slowly at first and then accelerate. Moving too rapidly creates problems for people near retirement age or who have recently retired and who have made their financial plans based on assumptions about the availability of Medicare coverage.

Raising the age of eligibility for Medicare would furthermore cause difficulties. Not all Americans are equally healthy at age 65. And while some Americans remain in the labor force or have generous retiree benefits at age 65, others struggle to make it to that age to qualify for Medicare. Nearly half of all persons aged 65 to 68 report themselves as retired. Many older persons who retire earlier or are disabled at, say, age 62 or 63, are in poor health and at present may not be able to purchase insurance on their own except at very high prices. And the two year waiting period for those with disabilities would preclude Medicare coverage even if these people qualified for Social Security.

To make this option less burdensome on those individuals, private insurance reform to assure access to the purchase of insurance would be critical. Alternatively, Medicare could allow individuals between ages 60 or 62 and age 68 to buy into Medicare. This would be analogous to the early retirement option under Social Security available at age 62—an option that will be retained even after the Social Security retirement age rises. Medicare would be available for those who must retire early. If this is also combined with some low-income protections and phased in slowly, the objections of critics could be effectively addressed.[29]

But although many persons aged 65 through 68 would be better able to afford higher premiums than are the very old, this is a rather imperfect way to differentiate among individuals on the basis of ability to pay. Within the 65 to 68 age group are also a substantial number of persons with modest incomes. For example, while a larger proportion of persons aged 69 and older have per capita incomes less than $10,000 per year (46.6 percent), over one-third (37.6 percent) of those aged 65 to 68 also have incomes below $10,000 (Census Bureau 1995). If income-relating of eligibility is the goal, it can be achieved more readily by means testing Medicare on the basis of income (or income-relating the premiums).

Means Testing Medicare

Thus, another possible dramatic change would be to fully means test Medicare, that is, making it available only to persons whose resources are below some prescribed limit. This is the ultimate extension of income-related premiums. Higher-income elderly and disabled persons could be offered the option of buying into the system at a non-subsidized rate or could be precluded from participating altogether. The former is likely to be the more desirable approach, however, since there might be savings to participants from the economies of scale and low administrative costs of Medicare even if no formal federal subsidy is involved. At present, people over 65 who are not eligible for Social Security benefits can buy into Part A for a premium of $261 per month, and a full actuarial premium for Part B would total about $146 per month.

The main justification for moving in the direction of means testing would be for budgetary savings. But some advocates of a means-tested approach also argue that public subsidies should not go to those with higher incomes. On the other hand, whereas the financing for Medicare is not progressive, the combination of benefits and taxes does result in a program in which higher-income beneficiaries pay a greater share of the costs through payroll taxes assessed over their working lives. For example, contributions from a salaried individual making $100,000 per year total $2,900, as compared to the $20,000 per year worker whose combined employee-employer contribution will be $580—both for the same benefit package.[30]

Eliminating high-income persons from eligibility would undermine some of the strong support for Medicare, precisely because it is a universal program. It would eliminate the image of a program into which everyone pays, but for which everyone also benefits. It would constitute a major shift in philosophy from a universal to a "welfare" program. Medicare would no longer be viewed as "middle-class."

A major practical concern with such an option is where the cutoff for eliminating the federal subsidy should be set. At what income is an elderly person capable of footing the bill for the full costs of Medicare? The Medicare premium for both Parts A and B totaled $4,913 in 1994 if an individual paid the full actuarial value. Other out-of-pocket spending would have averaged about $1,185, and premiums for private insurance would have raised the level even further. Together this total of over $6,200 would have consumed a substantial share of the income of most enrollees. Median per capita income—that is, the income level for the average elderly person—was less than $12,000. Certainly, at least half of the elderly would not be good candidates for paying for all their own care.

If policy were set so that average expenditures on health care did not total more than 15 percent of an individual's income, the cutoff for eligibility for Medicare would be set at over $40,000. If the figure used instead were 12 percent, the income cutoff would rise to over $50,000. These levels would mean that very few elderly persons would be excluded from Medicare. In 1992, only 4.2 percent of the elderly had per capita incomes in excess of $40,000 (Census Bureau 1995).[31] To obtain a higher share of the population (and hence generate more savings), the cutoff would need to begin at much lower incomes. For example, even if the cutoff were set at $20,000 per capita, only 18.2 percent of the elderly would be affected. And each year this calculation will look worse since health spending is rising faster than income.

To avoid the problem of an enormous "notch" where people just above an income cutoff receive nothing and people just below receive the full subsidy, a phaseout would be needed. For example, the subsidy could be reduced beginning with those whose incomes were $40,000 or more and then eliminated at, say, $60,000. The federal savings in that case would be substantially lower. The Concord Coalition (1994) proposal, for example, would begin reducing benefits for couples with incomes of about $31,000, but would only reach a reduction of 85 percent of benefits for those with incomes above $110,000.[32]

CONCLUSION

Medicare will undoubtedly undergo a number of changes to scale back spending in the near future. The combination of trust fund and deficit reduction pressures make it difficult—and undesirable—to delay making changes in Medicare. The challenge is in setting reasonable goals for savings and making wise choices regarding the array of available options. Some progress in cutting per capita spending growth will result from restricting provider payments and tightening oversight of the delivery of care, and should continue. But, given the problems that Medicare faces, it is inevitable that changes directly affecting beneficiaries will also be needed. Indeed, one way to achieve short-run savings is to require beneficiaries to pay more of the costs of their care, since program restructuring and other major changes need a longer time to be successfully implemented.

One of the biggest concerns is whether changes made to the program in the short run will substantially alter the nature of Medicare's insurance framework. Debate on this issue is likely to rage for some time. At the same time, like Social Security, Medicare needs to begin to look to the longer-term, when the baby boom generation will add substantial new pressures for change. Restructuring, changes in the age of eligibility for benefits, and new revenue sources all need to be analyzed and debated. Moreover, choices made in the next decade will influence what is possible and reasonable for the long term as well.

Notes

1. Much of the descriptive information on Medicare contained here can be found in more detail in Moon (1993).

2. In 1988, the passage of the Medicare Catastrophic Coverage Act (MCCA) began to change this homogeneity with two major provisions. The first was the introduction of an income-related premium on top of the existing flat premium for Part B of Medicare (which has since been repealed), and the second was in the form of special protections for low-income persons. The first of these was repealed in 1989, and while the second part is still in place, it is run through Medicaid.

3. Much in the same way that Social Security benefits have been raised over time to reflect overall higher standards of living, Medicare has mostly kept up with mainstream medical care received by persons of all ages, leading to greater use of services. Quality improvements, however, do affect the value of benefits.

4. This issue is discussed in more detail later in this chapter, but it would represent a major shift in the nature of the program. The terms *defined benefits* and *defined contributions* are most often used in connection with private pensions, and the meaning is somewhat different in this context. Essentially, those arguing for defined contributions are saying that the federal government can no longer afford to ensure that it will pay enough to continue a prescribed health insurance benefit package (the defined benefit), because costs of such insurance are rising so rapidly.

5. Actually, as noted in chapter 4, Social Security would be cut under the guise of a technical adjustment to the index used to set the cost-of-living adjustment (COLA).

6. Another argument used to justify such large changes in Medicare is that the program will still grow over time. There is considerable controversy over whether this should then be called a cut. But many analysts argue that if the growth is not sufficient to maintain the program, it is legitimate to refer to this as a cut (Moon 1995).

7. This organization of Medicare is largely a historical artifact. For more discussion, see Moon (1993).

8. Stop-loss protections refer to upper-bound limits placed on the amount that individuals will be required to pay in total cost sharing.

9. Medicaid, which was passed at the same time as Medicare, is a program targeted on persons with low incomes who meet certain eligibility criteria. Since this is a joint federal/state program, specifics of the program vary across the states, including how comprehensive is the coverage for elderly persons.

10. This was part of the Medicare Catastrophic legislation of 1988 and survived the repeal of some of the other portions.

11. Historically, the number of beneficiaries has grown at an average rate of about 1.9 percent since 1982 and even faster before that, explaining part of the high growth rates in spending (U.S. House 1994).

12. Since our emphasis in this volume is on the beneficiary, we do not discuss provider cuts at length. Extensive discussions of such proposals can be found elsewhere (Physician Payment Review Commission 1994; Prospective Payment Asessment Commission 1994; Smith 1992), although it is important to note that beneficiaries can be affected by provider cuts, particularly when they are very large (Moon 1993). That is, if cuts in provider payments are applied only to the Medicare program, doctors and hospitals may become increasingly reluctant to treat Medicare patients. They may thus reduce the time spent with patients or lower the quality of care delivered as part of cost-saving efforts in response to lower pay.

13. Indeed, Medicare will find it difficult to adopt new techniques for improving oversight if administrative budgets are severely cut in the future.

14. One difficulty, however, is that an increase in the Part B premium, which is one of the best ways to require more beneficiary contributions, does nothing to help the Part A trust fund problem.

15. That part of the Catastrophic Coverage legislation was later repealed, but added an income-related supplement on top of the basic premium. It was to rise gradually with income and reach a maximum of $800 per year for individuals with incomes above about $40,000 and for couples with incomes above about $70,000.

16. Part A receives the tax revenue on 35 percent of Social Security (i.e., the new revenues added in 1993). This was discussed in more detail in chapter 4. This provision may, however, be repealed, since it is part of the tax package passed by the House of Representatives early in 1995.

17. At present, the QMB program creates a "notch" in which persons with income $1 below the cutoff are eligible for full protection, while those with income $1 above that cutoff receive no help. A phaseout of this benefit would thus improve its equity.

18. Indeed, there are now proposals to begin income-relating (or even fully means testing, as described later in this chapter) at much lower income thresholds. For example, Peter Peterson (1993) has proposed beginning the threshold cutoff for phasing out Medicare (and Social Security) eligibility at about $35,000 of income (with the actual amount tied to the national family median income). This proposal would affect many more people—and raise much greater revenues.

19. Since the QMB program is now part of Medicaid, and because many states were traditionally reluctant to add this to their programs, some of the low participation in the QMB program would likely be helped simply by shifting it to the Medicare program. In that case, we assume that participation would rise to 65 percent of all eligibles. This change also means that the federal government would have to bear costs that are now the responsibility of states.

20. A formal cost estimate would also have to provide adjustments for phasing in such a change and the higher administrative costs likely to be associated with an income-related premium. But our figures are reasonably consistent with CBO estimates.

21. These are shown as increases in Medicare "liabilities," assuming that, except for those who have QMB protections, each beneficiary bears the full burden of these increases. For each income or age group, this is a reasonable representation of actual burdens for those with no private insurance or for those who buy Medigap. Those with employer-subsidized benefits would likely pay only a portion of this increase. In practice, the approximately one-third of the elderly with this subsidized insurance have higher incomes on average (Moon 1995).

22. Many analysts believe that most of the inappropriate growth in Medicare has occurred among these less-skilled services (Kenney and Moon 1995).

23. The OASI trust fund is predicted to be exhausted in 2030, compared to 2002 for Part A of Medicare (Board of Trustees, Federal HI Trust Fund 1995; Board of Trustees, Federal OASDI Trust Funds 1995).

24. Most of this new revenue could come as a shift out of Social Security, but because there is no upper limit on wages for the Medicare portion of the FICA tax, some of the revenue would represent a net increase in taxation.

25. Again, this is comparable to how Social Security is now treated in the tax code. In that case, the thresholds are $25,000 for single individuals and $32,000 for couples. These thresholds limit substantially the number of elderly and disabled persons who are taxed on their Social Security benefits.

26. Medical savings accounts essentially combine a catastrophic insurance plan with a deductible savings account in which funds are set aside to help pay the large deductible in the insurance plan.

27. For example, one way to select on the basis of risk is to appeal to the higher end of the income scale, where individuals tend to be healthier on average. Offering special access to the most expensive providers of care and stressing amenities might result in relatively high-cost plans, but ones that do not necessarily offer services that would attract a sicker population.

28. As yet, however, we have seen little movement in that direction; indeed, the age of retirement has steadily lowered over time.

29. Coordination with health care reform is particularly critical in this area. For example, some proposals would deal explicitly with early retirees through the employment-based system. In that case, lowering the Medicare eligibility age would not be an

issue. But if there were no extensions to assure coverage to persons in their 60s, making special arrangements for younger retirees might be crucial.

30. Actually, this results in an even more progressive package than the Social Security benefit, which does result in higher payments to those with higher incomes.

31. Options to eliminate Medicare for the very well off are effectively symbolic gestures that save little, at least initially. For example, just 2 percent of households with heads over age 65 have incomes above $100,000 (Census Bureau 1993a).

32. The Concord Coalition (1994) proposal identified the initial cutoff as $40,000, but that amount includes the actuarial value of Medicare benefits, which totaled over $4,000 per person in 1994.

Chapter Six

MEDICAID AND LONG-TERM CARE

The major Democratic proposals offered in the health care reform debate of 1994 all contained at least a minor expansion of public support for long-term care services, recognizing the need for additional help for the elderly and disabled in this area. Indeed, the inadequacies of our current long-term care system, particularly problems with Medicaid, are taken as a given by those who study this area. However, only one of the major health proposals in 1994—the so-called single-payer plan—offered a comprehensive long-term care benefit. The problem was essentially one of cost. Reluctance to raise new taxes or impose major new burdens on the public sector meant that few policymakers were willing to propose the $80 billion per year in new public spending required to fully cover long-term care services. Instead, the tactic was to offer limited expansions phased in very slowly over time. In contrast, Republican proposals generally ignored long-term care issues altogether or advocated only tax benefits for purchase of private insurance.

Any substantial improvement of our current long-term care system would require new public dollars either to expand Medicaid or add whole new benefits. But in an environment of cutting government spending, any expansion of long-term care services will be dictated by what resources are available and how to limit the nature of any entitlement. Resources freed up from Social Security and Medicare, as described in chapters 4 and 5, might be funneled into this effort, but may not be enough to make substantial inroads, particularly if most of the cuts are channeled into deficit reduction. Nonetheless, this chapter examines the current system and its inadequacies in order to begin to establish priorities for improvements in long-term care. We also explore various alternatives for limited expansions and the accompanying requirements for new resources.

THE CURRENT LONG-TERM CARE SYSTEM

Although the options for persons with disabilities are changing rapidly in the United States, care for older persons with the severest disabilities continues to occur in traditional institutional settings. The 1990 U.S. Census found that 1.77 million persons were in nursing homes in 1989, with most of them over the age of 65 (U.S. Department of Commerce 1993). The share of the population in nursing homes has been declining, however, while use of formal home and community-based services has grown. These expanding areas of service use may be home-delivered services or adult day care and other activities in settings outside the home. Data from 1984 indicated that just 30 percent of all persons with at least one limitation in activities of daily living (ADLs)—the most commonly used measure of disability—used home and community based services (Keenan 1988). In just three years, that figure rose to 41 percent (Agency for Health Care Policy and Research 1990). Projections of service use in the early 1990s indicate further dramatic expansions.

At present, long-term care is funded mainly by the federal/state Medicaid program and by individuals and their families. Other public programs, such as Medicare, play only a limited role. Over the last decade, private insurance has emerged as another means for spreading the risk of long-term care. Today, about 3.4 million Americans have purchased private insurance policies (Coronel and Fulton 1995).[1] However, policies that promise adequate protection against likely costs (a standard many do not meet) are not affordable by the vast majority of those senior citizens most in need of protection. The Health Insurance Association of America estimated the annual cost of such a policy at $2,525 for a 65-year-old in 1990 and $7,713 for a 79-year-old (Coronel and Fulton 1995).[2] And part of the "cost" of making such insurance affordable is precluding anyone with a long list of health problems from purchasing policies. Further, acceptance of the purchase of this new type of private insurance is bound to be slow. It will be many years before companies can point to a successful track record in this area, since there is likely to be a long lag between purchase of insurance and payment of benefits. Indeed, a number of analysts have argued that the public is responding rationally by not purchasing private long-term care insurance (Pauly 1990).

Since costs often exceed $35,000 per year for nursing home services and can be well over $15,000 per year for extensive home care services, these expenses can be devastating to families who lack private insurance. For that reason, many Americans ultimately turn for help to the Medicaid program.

Medicaid

The Medicaid program, which was originally established to help low-income families meet acute-care needs, has become the most important public program providing long-term care.[3] And since it was not designed to play such a role, it is not surprising that almost no one expresses satisfaction with the long-term care benefits provided by Medicaid. Despite current public expenditures of over $44 billion on that part of Medicaid—$25.5 billion of which goes to elderly persons (Liska et al. 1995), many gaps and inequities remain.

Medicaid provides mostly nursing home coverage, and eligibility is limited to individuals who have spent down their income and assets to very low levels.[4] It essentially offers protection after catastrophe has already occurred. Middle-income people benefit from the program, but only once they have already devoted most of their resources to paying for care. Medicaid has been characterized as insurance whereby the deductible is your lifetime savings and the coinsurance is your annual income. Nonetheless, since it is the only public program to offer substantial coverage to those with disabilities, Medicaid has been used more and more by middle-class families who find the costs of long-term care prohibitively expensive. It is no longer confined to a minority of persons with low incomes.

For many American families, the spend-down requirements represent a very unpalatable option, and have led to systematic efforts to subvert these requirements. Policymakers have become alarmed at the resulting growth and perceived manipulation of the system—for example, by those who have substantial resources but choose to dispose of them in order to qualify for eligibility. Although this abuse may not be widespread, it is substantial enough to create considerable concern about fairness. And, in some areas of the country, such as New York, the feeling is that the abuses are large and come from those with very high incomes. Evidence on asset transfers, not surprisingly, is difficult to obtain. However, a 1993 General Accounting Office study found that whereas one out of every eight applicants for Medicaid had transferred assets within 30 months of the application, one-third of these transfers totaled less than $10,000.

Recent changes in the law to limit transfers of assets reflect a direct response to these perceived abuses. But these new state activities in areas such as estate recovery programs may penalize most those who are least sophisticated, while failing to curb abuses by those with the most advanced legal advice. Moreover, states are often reluctant to press for estate recovery activities, for example, because of the often negative response of the public. Making everyone use their own assets before becoming eligible for benefits sounds better in theory; in practice, enforcing such behavior has proven to be problematic. Thus, the welfare nature of the program creates problems for both government and the public. The bottom-line issue is whether enough is saved through these stringent spend-down requirements to justify the dissatisfaction and abuse that have developed around Medicaid.[5]

The rapid growth in the costs of long-term care have also led states to focus on holding down the number of nursing home beds, to limit reimbursement for nursing homes, and to restrict their programs to institutional settings as additional ways to limit spending. For example, limits on home care programs reflect the fact that placing bounds on services is more difficult in a setting where individuals remain comfortably at home. Such individuals would see government-provided services as a benefit with few costs and hence seek more services whenever possible. In contrast, having to make a major decision to move to an institutional environment is itself an impediment to demanding such care. This, perhaps more than any other reason, is why Medicaid policy continues to be dominated by nursing home care. For example, in 1992, almost 90 percent of all Medicaid long-term care dollars for the elderly were for nursing home services (Coughlin et al. 1994).

Prospects for the Future

If the current picture of long-term care financing looks bleak, the future looks even worse. Projections are that the elderly population will grow by 73 percent in the next 30 years (Taueber 1992). The population over age 85 who are most likely to need long-term care is expected to more than double in that period, growing by 115 percent. The hope is that at the same time that we increase our longevity, we will make important advances against diseases of old age such as Alzheimer's as well as other disabilities. Until recently, research seemed to indicate that longer lives have not translated into healthier lives, indicating a substantial increase in the need for long-term care (Guralnick 1991). But a more recent study by Manton, Corder, and Stallard (1993) indicated that some age-adjusted declines in disability may now be occurring. This is an area where considerable further attention is needed, since it will affect the affordability of various long-term care strategies. Nonetheless, the incidence of disability will rise as the population ages with the demographic changes ahead, but perhaps not by as much as the simple aging of the population would indicate.

Private insurance coverage may continue to grow, as future older Americans with higher incomes are better able to afford its costs or to purchase it at younger ages. However, even optimistic projections of private insurance growth suggest that 25 years from now, purchase of private insurance will still be confined to higher-income elderly persons and will do little to mitigate the potential catastrophic costs of long-term care for most senior citizens (Wiener et al. 1994). As a result, Wiener and colleagues have estimated that with no change in policy, the demands on the welfare-based Medicaid program will rise with the growth in the elderly population. And these pressures will occur at a time when the Medicaid program is slated for a $182 billion spending reduction.

WHY IS A PUBLIC-SECTOR SOLUTION NEEDED?

It makes little sense for individuals to rely only on their savings to meet long-term care needs. Not everyone will require such care, but when they do, it can be very expensive. In a sense, this is the perfect "insurable" event, in which the risks ought to be shared across a large group. But the private sector has been slow to develop such insurance despite a well-demonstrated need.

Why can't individuals simply seek long-term care insurance products through the private market? Insurers are understandably cautious about marketing products where the liabilities will not be known for many years. Indeed, it is prudent for insurers to operate conservatively so they are certain to have the resources to pay benefits in the future. This conservativeness, combined with the costs of marketing and selling to a largely nongroup market, may make the price too high for many persons aged 65 and over. Further, private insurers often offer coverage only to individuals in good health at the time of enrollment (Rice, Thomas, and Weissert 1990). In addition to current disability, individuals with hypertension, arthritis, or any history of heart disease, diabetes, or recent hospitalization may be screened out. As yet, there is little evidence that such factors are actually good indicators of later need for long-term care, but individuals with such medical histories are nonetheless unlikely to be able to purchase individual long-term care insurance policies. For this reason, many supporters of private insurance stress the importance of encouraging younger persons to purchase insurance.

Thus, there will always be gaps left by private insurance approaches. Even if tax benefits are added to encourage purchase of insurance, many moderate-income families cannot and should not purchase such coverage. Their assets are low, and they would effectively be lowering their standard of living for many years to buy policies that may not protect them over time.[6] Thus, if we wish to expand the availability of long-term care services for low- and moderate-income individuals, a public component must be at least part of the solution. The Medicaid approach, which is not insurance, but, rather, support after individuals have depleted their resources, is widely disliked. It offers help, but too late to provide the same type of protection offered by insurance. At a minimum, considerable expansions of Medicaid would be necessary to fill in the gaps with a private insurance approach, however.

HOW COMPREHENSIVE SHOULD PUBLIC LONG-TERM CARE COVERAGE BE?

Despite widespread agreement that long-term care would best be covered by some form of insurance and that government must play a role in developing that insurance, there is disagreement as to the balance between the public and private sectors. As in acute care, options range from strategies that promote private insurance while limiting the public's role to that of a safety net for the poor, to strategies for developing a universal social insurance system to protect all Americans, regardless of income, for long-term care needs. In between are strategies that would provide limited social insurance—combining social insurance for some benefits with a public/private partnership for others—and offering government-subsidized insurance, either public or private in nature.

As recently as the mid-1980s, a comprehensive program of social insurance for long-term care was being seriously discussed. Such a program would guarantee to all disabled persons access to a nursing home and to home and community-based services as needed. But the high and escalating price tags for long-term care, coupled with the enormous growth in the acute-care portions of Medicare and Medicaid, have moved the debate away from such solutions. Indeed, the prospects in 1995 for $182 billion in savings from Medicaid over seven years suggest that less, rather than more, benefits from Medicaid may be available to meet the long-term care needs of the elderly. Nonetheless, it is useful to consider some modest improvements in public long-term care services.

We begin with an examination of the advantages and disadvantages of a full social insurance program, but devote most of our analysis to less-comprehensive approaches. The antitax, antigovernment sentiment of the 1990s suggests that any expansion of long-term care would begin gradually. For policymaking, one of the toughest challenges is to find reasonable ways to move incrementally and at moderate cost. This is a tough assignment in an area where even modest expansions can be quite expensive.

Comprehensive Long-term Care Coverage

In the aggregate, the financial resources required to provide long-term care services to all sobers even the most sympathetic legislators. In an era of fiscal austerity and concern over reducing the federal budget deficit, enacting a public, comprehensive long-term care system is now generally viewed as beyond our collective means. Nevertheless, considerable support exists for such a program, including important arguments for an entitlement approach.

Society as a whole is now bearing much of the cost of long-term care, but in ways that place enormous burdens on a few. Some of these are very visible costs: the $44 billion that Medicaid spends on long-term care each year, and the even larger amount that individuals and families pay. There are also invisible costs in the sacrifices that families make and in the unmet needs that result in suffering and reduced quality of life for those with unmet needs.

A universal program would help ensure access to quality care for all Americans. Leaving the current system intact or encouraging private insurance will assure two distinct worlds of long-term care services and delivery. Already many providers concentrate on the "private" market, discriminating against Medicaid patients. As a welfare program, payments are low in many areas, and providers know that private-pay patients will bring in more revenues and greater profits. Naturally, private-pay patients are preferred to Medicaid patients, often resulting in the seemingly contradictory findings of empty beds, yet waiting lists under Medicaid.

A comprehensive program could also be efficient. Social Security and Medicare have both proven to be very effective in holding administrative costs to a minimum. For example, Medicare is able to return about $0.96 in benefits for every $1 of financing. A public system would also clearly benefit from having the largest possible risk pool over which to spread both risks and costs. Moreover, a public program like Medicare has no marketing or advertising expenses. Finally, the delivery system for any long-term care program will be an essential element in determining whether needs are met at a reasonable cost. A single system for reimbursing providers offers opportunities to mold an as-yet-undeveloped delivery system and to use prudent purchasing to hold down costs of care.

But moving to a national universal system could lead to inflexibility. Services now vary dramatically from location to location in the United States. What works well in Buffalo, New York, may not be easily transported to a small town in Arizona. Long-term care likely does not need to be as standardized as the acute-care system in order to be efficient and of high quality. Thus, fitting everything into one mold may not be the best approach, and could add to costs over time.

A universal system undeniably would result in increased costs of long-term care both in terms of public spending and in terms of the resources society devoted to such care. Those who now postpone or avoid obtaining services because of the fear of being on welfare or the inability to qualify would become eligible. In addition, expansion of covered services into community and home-based settings would encourage users who wish to avoid institutionalization at all costs. Although such expansion may be politically difficult, it should not be decried as bad simply because costs would rise. Indeed, meeting unmet needs should be a goal of an expanded system, and some increase in expenditures on nursing home and home and community services should be welcomed. But no one should assume that efficiencies that might be obtained from a public program would offset these new expenses.

One of the most compelling arguments against a comprehensive expansion of Medicare or a separate program to cover long-term care is the issue of cost. It is hard to advocate spending an additional $80 billion on long-term care when Medicare is facing the requirement to yield seven-year savings of over $270 billion to help reduce the deficit. Since the elderly are increasingly viewed as a "privileged" group, expanding benefits to this population before solving other problems may be politically untenable. Indeed, many critics of expanded long-term care protection argue that it would mainly serve to protect the assets of the upper middle class and preserve inheritances. If so, this would not be the most efficient or desirable use of public dollars.

Finally, the current political environment is one of considerable distrust of the government, suggesting that a broad new public program might not be well received even if funds were available.

Strategies for Limiting the Scope of Solutions

But political pendulums do swing, and long-term care services remain an extremely popular area of possible expansion. Even if we move in the next few years to again consider new spending on domestic programs, such efforts would likely begin slowly. Thus, options for expanding long-term care needs must include limits on eligibility and benefits in order to keep the scope of any new program manageable. Six different strategies could be employed to limit such liability. Although many of these could be used in combination in a new benefit program, the first two are essentially mutually exclusive approaches.

The first way to limit expenditures would use the welfare-based approach of Medicaid and means-test access. This limits eligibility for services based on the financial situation of disabled persons, usually in terms of both income and assets. Whereas this approach concentrates eligibility on those least able to pay, if stringent, it could result in making persons ineligible who still could not afford the costs of long-term care. That is, if income and asset limits are low enough to substantially limit the number of disabled persons who qualify, many who need services would be excluded. For example, estimates of President Clinton's home and community-based care plan assumed that only 30 percent of those eligible would have had incomes over 250 percent of poverty. But at that income level, long-term care services are still not affordable. Medicaid deals with this problem by establishing eligibility on the basis of income *after* health care spending has been subtracted. In other words, persons will ultimately get government help, but only after they have spent down their incomes and assets to a low level. Allowing people to spend down to eligibility means that many more are eligible than would appear to be the case by looking just at the income and asset limits. Ultimately, most older Americans would qualify for help, but only after spending down all their resources.

A second type of limitation (in lieu of means testing) would require substantial out-of-pocket contributions by those receiving the care—often in relationship to their incomes. Thus, eligibility would begin immediately for disabled persons (requiring no period of spending down assets) and would extend further up the income scale, but higher-income persons would have to contribute to the costs of care.

This cuts costs directly through the sharing of expenses, and may limit demand for care when recipients must pay something for the services received. It is less burdensome than a full spend-down requirement, and hence may be somewhat less subject to the gaming that often occurs under the traditional Medicaid approach. But since it is less of a burden on individuals, it is more costly to the public sector than is a full means-tested approach.

Costs may also be limited by restricting eligibility to those with severe disabilities. It is easier to make a case for providing services to meet the needs of the severely disabled population. That is, this approach may satisfy concerns of policymakers that people with mild disabilities might otherwise take advantage of homemaker and personal care services that they do not need. Restricting eligibility to persons with limitations in at least three activities of daily living, rather than two, would cut the number of potential elderly eligibles by about 50 percent (U.S. House 1993). At the same time, however, this also precludes early intervention for disabled persons whose functional limitations might otherwise be reduced or eliminated. Advocates of broader long-term care coverage often make the analogy to preventive services for acute care. Moreover, many of the exciting innovations in long-term care are occurring for the less severely disabled who are still able to retain considerable independence. Many such individuals, unfortunately, would not be eligible for benefits if such benefits were restricted to those with the greatest impairments.

A fourth way to reduce the costs of new coverage is to limit the types of benefits offered—usually by expanding just home and community-based services, for example. Home and community-based services are the most undeveloped part of long-term care. Medicaid paid just $2.7 billion for home health services for the elderly in 1993 (Liska et al. 1995). Thus, limiting benefits to these areas would not only help to expand the program but would phase it in more slowly as an infrastructure develops and the supply of workers and services grows. Even a modest $3 billion to $4 billion in new spending per year would represent a large expansion for home health. On the other hand, what people fear most are the crippling costs of institutional care. There would be considerable sentiment to expand this area of protection further. In addition, any strategy that places arbitrary limits on how care may be delivered will likely distort choices and lead to inefficiency. Problems we have seen with coordinating acute and long-term care would likely be replicated in discontinuities within the long-term care sector.

A fifth strategy would focus on controlling payments to care providers. This could be accomplished by price controls or fee schedules for services to limit the rate of growth of payments. Moreover, allowing less-formal care to be provided and thus avoiding expensive certified agencies is another way to potentially limit provider reimbursements. Some critics of this strategy claim that we likely get what we pay for, and if payments are too restrictive, quality of care will suffer. Low payments under the Medicaid program implicitly rely upon cross-subsidies from patients who pay higher private rates. If long-term care is expanded, the share of public-to-private-pay patients would rise, making it difficult to maintain low payment levels. Another area just beginning to be explored in long-term care is that of possible savings from developing managed-care strategies for services, but it will likely take many years before substantial gains will be achieved there.

Finally, some proposals place fixed limits on the amount of dollars allowed for the program. For example, the federal government could either give grants to states or offer a matching program with an upper bound on what the federal government is willing to contribute. This is in contrast to the open-ended nature of entitlement programs that would otherwise expand automatically with eligibility and service needs. A variation on this approach is to combine broad eligibility standards with fixed appropriations. These so-called capped entitlements are intended to avoid the problem of expenses rising directly in response to beneficiary demand, while assuring open-ended eligibility to the disabled. If states or other entities are left to administer such a program, they will have to find ways to live within budgets. This may create a dilemma for states if expectations rise faster than the dollars to pay for services. This approach does not solve the problem; it just shifts it to another level of government. On the other hand, some states, like Oregon, have proven to be very skilled in providing innovative programs with limited funds.

Each of these strategies for limiting the scope of any long-term care expansion thus has advantages and disadvantages. Any program that seeks to provide only modest expansions in long-term care must adopt several of these strategies (although there is no easy way to keep spending very low). But these strategies do not necessarily define what a specific option for expanding long-term care would look like.

MODELS FOR LIMITED EXPANSION

There are basically two models for limited expansion of long-term care services. The first approach would build on the existing Medicaid program, correcting its most important weaknesses but maintaining essentially a means-tested or at least an income-tested approach. The second way to provide limited services would be through a restricted social insurance undertaking. Both of these approaches would allow—and perhaps encourage—the development of private insurance to wrap around these benefits. These two approaches are analyzed in more detail in the subsection following.

Medicaid Expansion

Some argue that government can most efficiently promote long-term care services by facilitating the expansion of private long-term care insurance and expanding Medicaid for those who cannot afford such private coverage. This approach would essentially seek to expand coverage by closing the gap in the middle by expansions at each end of the income distribution. That is, more low-income people would be aided by Medicaid, and subsidies or other enticements to buy private insurance would move the feasibility of that approach down the income scale to attract middle-income families. The biggest challenge of this approach is to find ways to make such a system meet in the middle so that large groups of the population are not left out. But the two pieces are, to some extent, at odds, making a reasonable system difficult to maintain.

A variety of ways to expand purchase of private insurance have been suggested. For example, subsidies, through tax credits or provision of enhanced public protections for those who buy insurance, could promote purchase of private insurance by moderate-income families. These subsidies would help to lower the costs of insurance, and they should be phased out at higher incomes. A few states are now experimenting with promoting private insurance by expediting Medicaid eligibility for those who purchase such policies. The private policies are kept more affordable by covering only a limited time period. After that period, individuals could become eligible for Medicaid without spending down all of their assets. This preferential public coverage, added at the "back end" of a stay, would mean that for purchase of more modest insurance, individuals would get full protection for a long nursing home stay. Variations of this approach are being tried in several states, particularly New York and Connecticut (Mahoney 1990). Proponents argue that in the long run this should save Medicaid costs, since people will remain off the roles longer. Detractors worry that this approach is more likely to appeal to those with higher incomes, and will still remain unaffordable for persons with more modest resources. As yet, this approach has not attracted many Americans. It seems that those who consider buying private insurance do not find the ability to access Medicaid in the future appealing; indeed, they may be buying insurance to explicitly avoid having to depend upon Medicaid. Public education could also help to facilitate growth in the number of people purchasing long-term care insurance. Furthermore, public standards and oversight to ensure adequate value for the dollar and other consumer protections in the developing marketplace could reduce some of the fears about abuses.

Subsidies for long-term care insurance would begin to bring in more moderate-income families, but Medicaid would also need to be improved in a number of critical ways to make this a viable option for meeting the needs of most such families. As already mentioned, Medicaid's coverage of long-term care was not an explicit goal of the original program. It moved rather haphazardly into this area, and many aspects of the program are problematic. Consequently, Medicaid expansion may sound like a minimalist approach, but in practice could be quite expensive. For example, Medicaid's coverage of services is distorted, placing too much emphasis on nursing home services and not enough on home and community-based care. This lack of expansion is not accidental; states, which control the Medicaid program, often limit these other services in order to slow the growth in this part of the program. Similarly, payment levels to providers are often low, causing providers to discriminate against Medicaid patients and resist making beds available.

The welfare nature of Medicaid with its stringent income and asset limits is also problematic—discouraging some from participating and encouraging others to game the system to become eligible. Relaxing the income and asset rules could help, but may not be enough to resolve the issue.[7] Moreover, establishing expanded eligibility for Medicaid raises a conflict with private insurance expansion. If the rules are too liberal, this may discourage individuals from purchasing private insurance, and choose instead to rely on Medicaid. On the other hand, if the restrictions are too severe, moderate-income families will be caught in the middle—unable to afford private insurance premiums but penalized substantially if they must rely on Medicaid. Again, it is the families in the middle who will likely lose.

Complicating all of these other factors is the issue of state variability in the Medicaid program. Since states determine what the programs will look like and then receive matching funds, the resulting coverage of long-term care varies enormously across the United States. For example, per capita annual expenditures on long-term care varied from $497 in New York to $76 in California (Liska et al. 1995). The variation is even more dramatic in the case of home and community-based services: $124 in New York versus $2 in California.[8] Partly this reflects variations in states' abilities to pay, but it also captures their willingness to support substantial long-term care benefits under Medicaid. Establishing national standards or even minimums would require considerable new federal resources and likely an overhaul in the operation of this joint federal/state program.

Thus, this approach to long-term care poses many problems. Even with subsidies, private insurance would remain too expensive for most elderly people to purchase without substantial financial sacrifice. Subsidies for the purchase of insurance could disproportionately benefit the better-off relative to the moderate-income elderly. Even more important, such a strategy will be inadequate to achieve universal protection against long-term care risks—unless the subsidies and Medicaid expansion were much greater than what is usually proposed and unless even stronger restrictions are placed on states—an unlikely prospect at a time when we are discussing more discretion by states, not less. Even optimistic projections indicate that it will be decades before significant numbers of elderly have the resources to purchase private long-term care insurance. Moderate-income persons will be the ones who remain outside this system. In the meantime, inadequacies and impoverishment would persist. And even 40 years from now, long-term care insurance would remain too expensive for more than half the elderly to purchase at a price less than 5 percent of income (Pepper Commission 1990).[9]

Pursuing such a strategy seems ironic given the inadequacy of using a combination of Medicaid and private insurance to cover acute care for the population under age 65. To repeat the nation's experience in health insurance—to intentionally build a system that will inevitably leave out vast numbers of Americans, entail innumerable inefficiencies, and produce uncontrolled increases in health care costs—is to invite problems in the future. The gaps that our mixed private and Medicaid system creates for the under-age-65 population in the acute-care insurance environment are analogous to what could develop in long-term care. And just as the acute-care environment can be criticized for gaps in coverage, a mixed private-public approach to long-term care could fail to protect the most vulnerable group—men and women of moderate incomes.

Even more problematic is looking to Medicaid at a time when Congress is seeking $182 billion in savings from this program. It seems likely that many states will cut back on spending in areas where expansions are needed. Payment levels to nursing homes and experimental home care programs may be particularly at risk, for example (Holahan et al., forthcoming). And if states are given a free hand, variability in public long-term care benefits may increase rather than decrease. Nonetheless, if Medicaid remains the main source of public spending on long-term care, improvements at the margin may be our only viable option for the near term. In that case, the challenge will be to prioritize what aspects of the program can most successfully be enhanced.

Limited Social Insurance

Rather than putting substantial resources into an expanded Medicaid program and subsidies for private insurance, a new, albeit restricted, social insurance program to cover some long-term care services could be created. The logical area for such a program is usually thought to be home and community-based services, since this area is now relatively underserved by Medicaid, and this was the approach taken in a number of the Democratic reform plans in 1994. The goal of such a new program would be to preserve standards of living for those who reside in the community. Home care would be provided as a social insurance benefit. Most users of such care have relatively low incomes and assets, so making coverage universal would add little to program costs. Moreover, home care users need to retain a considerable share of their assets and income, since they remain at home and must meet the demands of routine costs of living. Since home care is considerably less expensive than nursing home coverage, its expansion would more be affordable.[10]

Such a program could begin slowly and expand over time using some of the savings from Social Security and Medicare, and perhaps redirecting some of current federal spending in Medicaid on home care. Expansion of this program over time would, however, likely require an inflow of additional public support.

Coverage for nursing home care could be left intact under Medicaid or be expanded in a limited way. Expansion could come from relaxing Medicaid's eligibility rules—perhaps eliminating asset spend-down requirements, for example. If other parts of Medicaid spending are reduced—for example by moving the Qualified Medicare Beneficiary program to Medicare (see chapter 5)—funds could be freed up for such an improvement. This would be contingent on retaining a federal presence in Medicaid, however.

These limited expansions offer the potential for spreading at least some of the risks of long-term care costs, while targeting public resources to the low- and moderate-income population. They also leave a role for private insurance to serve those with substantial resources who would wish further protection.

CONCLUSION

Although no "solution" to the problem of long-term care appears to be on the horizon, some increase in public support (either direct and/ or through tax relief) could help to ease some of the most egregious hardships that our current system imposes. The lack of a commitment to public financing means that we will retain a patchwork approach that leaves serious gaps and inequities. And if Medicaid becomes a block-granted program subsisting on even more limited federal contributions, unmet need for long-term care services will grow—particularly in some states. Nonetheless, some expansion of long-term care should be possible, financed in part by economies in other programs even in this era of fiscal austerity. But to do so will require an effort counter to much of the current thinking in the area of entitlement policy.

Notes

1. This is an estimate of the number of policies purchased to date, some of which undoubtedly have lapsed.

2. This assumes a $100 per day nursing home or a $50 per day home health care policy with 5 percent inflation protection and a nonforfeiture benefit.

3. Other public programs offer more modest coverage. Medicare, the acute-care program for the aged and disabled, covers less than 5 percent of long-term care expenses. Indeed, many elderly persons are surprised to discover how little Medicare covers when they are in need of long-term care. Skilled nursing facility benefits and home health care services are offered by Medicare, but are limited to those with acute medical problems. They provide for transition care for persons after acute episodes. Social Services Block Grants and elderly nutrition programs of the Administration on Aging also offer limited benefits to those in need. But these are appropriated programs and are not very generously funded. Moreover, the Social Services Block Grants cover a variety of services, and long-term care must compete for a share of the total.

4. *Spend down* is a term used to refer to the requirement that before becoming eligible for nursing home coverage, an individual must use all of his or her assets above a certain cutoff to pay for care. And then after becoming asset eligible, the individual

must spend essentially most of his or her income each period before Medicaid will pay the balance.

5. This also suggests crucial lessons for those who advocate similar stringent means testing for Medicare and Social Security, for example.

6. That is, insurance of this sort offers a means for protecting assets.

7. Moderate moves in this direction—estimated to cost about $2.5 billion per year when fully phased in—were included in President Clinton's health reform plan.

8. Per capita numbers are used to control for general population size. Other types of adjustments, such as by number of elderly persons or number of elderly poor, continue to yield major differentials.

9. Early purchase of insurance makes it more affordable. But it also increases the risk of lapsing and receiving no benefits.

10. Home care is less expensive largely because it would be reserved for those less expensively served at home. For persons with very severe disabilities, comprehensive home care is actually more expensive than nursing home care. And if this area is expanded, more expensive patients who could be better served in nursing homes may seek to remain in the community.

Chapter Seven

A COMBINED APPROACH TO ENTITLEMENT REFORMS

Views on entitlement reform often devolve into two camps: advocates of locking the major entitlement programs for the elderly in place with no room for change, and those who would dramatically scale back the programs. Although both approaches may attract headlines and political attention, neither one protects the programs in realistic and equitable ways. Instead, the fundamental challenge should be to consider changes in these programs that will more equitably distribute benefits across individuals and across time.

An additional mistake made in much of the debate regarding entitlements and the elderly is to treat Social Security, Medicare, and Medicaid as fully separate programs. For example, some supporters view Social Security as essential and Medicare as expendable. And advocates for a long-term care social insurance benefit often take for granted the continuation of Social Security and Medicare regardless of the impact of expanding long-term care. However, the large and growing share of the federal budget devoted to entitlement programs for seniors suggests that we cannot expect to view each of these programs separately. In practice, there are already many important linkages.

This concluding chapter considers some trade-offs among Social Security, Medicare, and Medicaid's long-term care benefits, and proposes, as well, an approach for balancing these programs over time. We turn, first, to the reasons why each program might or might not receive preferential treatment and then suggest changes that meet the goals of a more streamlined and targeted set of benefits that could be sustained into the future.

WHERE SHOULD CHANGE OCCUR?

One of the first challenges of beginning to scale back entitlements for the elderly is to determine where to begin. Many supporters of Social

Security regard it as the most crucial benefit for older Americans because it is a major contributor to income, which in turn constitutes the most essential building block of economic well-being. Moreover, economists like to point out that this entitlement is received in cash and hence can be translated into any other benefit that its recipients wish—in contrast, for example, to the medical benefits provided under Medicare and Medicaid. Social Security is the oldest social insurance program in the United States and was viewed as the benefit most vital for senior citizens when a wide range of policies were debated in the 1930s.

But Social Security may also be the most amenable to change over time, since benefit amounts can be fine-tuned in ways that are more difficult with in-kind benefits. Small adjustments in the benefit formula, modest changes in the age of eligibility (or eligibility for full benefits), and changes in taxation of benefits can be accomplished with little disruption and without changing the program's basic philosophy. Indeed, these elements have already been subjected to adjustment. Moreover, the progressivity of the program can be carefully controlled to assure that reductions in average benefits affect mainly or exclusively higher-income groups.[1]

In the case of Medicare and Medicaid, it is difficult to find ways to subdivide the in-kind benefits incrementally. For example, Medicare's benefit could be redefined not as a basic insurance package but as a set dollar amount and allowed to grow only at a given rate, but that would essentially eliminate the in-kind nature of the benefit and change substantially the program. Another way to subdivide the benefit would be to means test Medicare, but, again, that would require a major change in the program's philosophy and a substantial new administrative mechanism to enforce these changes. Further, Medicare offers considerable economies of scale that make it less expensive per capita to provide insurance to all older persons than if provided on an individual or more limited basis. Finally, Medicare is already a more progressive benefit than Social Security because its value does not rise with the level of past contributions made to the program. High-wage contributors still receive the same basic benefit as those who contribute substantially less over their working lives.

Medicaid's long-term care benefit falls into a somewhat different category, since few analysts would argue that it is now too generous. It is already means tested and provides an incomplete set of benefits. Improvements in long-term care have been discussed as part of health care reform and as a standalone benefit for many years. But it may be unrealistic to expect expansion in this realm without some offsetting decreases elsewhere. Moreover, expansion into a new and potentially expensive area may be swimming upstream against a heavy current of pressure to cut back on government programs that disproportionately benefit older persons.

Another dimension to consider in beginning to change entitlements surrounds the health of the trust funds and other financing issues. The trust fund financing problems with Social Security are farther out on the horizon than the problems facing Medicare and Medicaid— a fact that could be argued either to support the ability to change Social Security slowly and methodically over time or to contend that we can postpone for some time any adjustments. Changes in the formula for new beneficiaries or increases in the age of eligibility for full retirement benefits can be phased in very gradually, without disrupting individuals' retirement planning and decision making. Moreover, that would allow some shifting of resources into the Medicare program or elsewhere in the intermediate term as the trust funds build up a larger balance over time. But it is also more difficult to achieve political consensus to change Social Security now when the crisis looms so far into the future.

On the other hand, the Medicare Part A benefit is now rising at a rate much faster than the growth in contributions into the trust fund, putting its financial status at considerable risk. Moreover, reductions in spending on Medicare are the centerpiece of congressional plans to reduce the federal budget deficit. Major changes do need to be made in the near future—although they could come on the revenue side as well as from reductions in spending. Holding the line on overall health care spending is likely to be a critical element in controlling government spending over time. But the issue here is how far cuts in benefits to recipients should go as a means for controlling growth and whether this is the preferred policy choice. If alterations in Medicare benefits must come in the next few years, an argument for exempting Social Security would be to first focus on Medicare, but reassure beneficiaries by holding Social Security out as "untouchable." Alternatively, Social Security could face changes as a way of moderating changes needed in Medicare.

Finally, the current long-term care benefits under Medicaid are likely to be scaled back if the 1996 budget outline passed by Congress is adhered to over the next seven years. Although much of the emphasis on planned reductions in Medicaid spending focuses on acute-care services, long-term care would also be affected given the magnitude of the reductions being planned. Reductions in this area represent less a judgment on whether we *should* engage in cutbacks and more a matter of whether we *will*.

WHERE SHOULD WE GO FROM HERE?

Our assessment of changes that ought to be made in entitlements for the elderly combines some scaling back of Social Security and Medicare (with some reordering of benefits to better target those in need), along with a limited effort to use some of those freed-up resources to improve long-term care. Despite the extremely negative political climate, some small expansion of revenues to help improve long-term care services ought to be honestly discussed as well.[2] We do not favor radical change that either refocuses the programs by privatizing Social Security or Medicare, or by means testing Medicare, for example. If a combination of more incremental options is employed, no one change need be extremely disruptive.

Reassuring skeptical Americans about the stability of the programs is not likely to occur in the context of proposing radical changes. Moreover, employing a range of smaller changes makes it feasible to ask for sacrifices from most Americans, thereby spreading the burdens and creating more of a sense of fairness. Analyses of what is necessary to place Social Security on a sound footing suggest that incremental changes will be sufficient even over the long run. And such a strategy allows changes to begin to be implemented while keeping open options for further change in the future.

But if there are to be more radical shifts, these should be reserved for the longer-term problems arising from anticipated demographic changes, and only after time has allowed better analysis and information and a more informed debate than has yet occurred. For example, the shifts in the private health care sector that now seem underway may alter the outlook for health care spending over time. But the jury is still out on the effects of managed care and competition. If these prove to be very promising areas, there is still plenty of time to more radically shift Medicare to take full advantage of any innovations that can only be accomplished in the private sector.

Social Security

Social Security is already a targeted program, since benefits vary in a progressive manner. Thus, we can use several of the mechanisms already in place, and simply change them at the margin. The first of these, taxation of Social Security benefits, offers the most carefully targeted change since it implicitly takes into account all the resources available to individuals—or at least the ones subject to the income tax. Benefits are reduced for those with the greatest ability to absorb such a cut. A reasonable alternative would subject at least 85 percent of benefits to taxation while moderately lowering the thresholds that exempt many beneficiaries from taxation. This change would require sacrifices from both current and future beneficiaries.

A second element affecting current beneficiaries as well as those yet to retire would be to place a dollar cap on the Social Security cost-of-living adjustment (COLA) so that people with higher benefits still get substantial COLAs, but ones slightly less than they receive under current law. We believe this to be a more reasonable approach than the across-the-board reductions in COLAS proposed as part of the 1996 federal budget.

Both increased taxation of benefits and a limit on the COLA would effectively increase the balance in the Social Security trust funds immediately—and might be thought of as changes that could free up some resources to moderate changes or even provide modest improvements in other entitlements for the elderly.[3] These might include improvements in the survivors' benefit under Social Security or bolstering financing for the medical benefits directed to the elderly.

The remaining changes in Social Security would mainly aid the longer-run outlook. First, changing the "bend points" or lowering the replacement rates in the formula for calculating benefits could modestly alter benefit levels for future retirees. Benefits could be made more progressive by making changes only at the upper end of the benefit range. As a result of these changes, the current limit on earnings subject to the payroll tax could also be raised without substantially increasing liabilities for future benefits, since the replacement rates for high-income workers would be quite low.[4]

A second change focused on the longer term would speed up the process of raising the eligibility age for full Social Security benefits. Currently, the law calls for all persons born between 1943 and 1954 to have age 66 as their normal retirement age; effectively, there is a moratorium on raising the eligibility age for 10 years. Instead, the formula's schedule could be advanced so that persons born in 1944 would have their normal retirement age at 66 years, 2 months. And in each succeeding year the retirement age would continue to rise. This would mean that the full change in retirement age to 67 could be accomplished by the year 2011 instead of 2022.

If needed, further increases in the eligibility age could occur in later years. This is controversial since its impact is less targeted; low-income workers in unpleasant jobs are often the ones who retire early, and thus this change is more likely to penalize them. But, this reform would not take effect for a long time, thus allowing most workers to change their behavior to adapt. And reduced benefits would still be available to younger retirees. Greater reliance on later retirement also should require a close look at the disability program to ensure that workers who cannot stay in the labor force because of poor health have access to Social Security disability benefits. Other policies that affect workers' ability and willingness to remain in the work force longer should also be scrutinized.

Increases in the age of eligibility for full benefits and possible small increases in the payroll tax (or even other tax revenue) might be used as levers to help assure the very long-run financial viability of the program. One consequence of beginning such a combination of changes sooner rather than later would be a buildup in the trust fund for Old-Age and Survivors Insurance (OASI) in the near term—a prospect that would also improve the federal deficit outlook or potentially offer some opportunities for private investment of the trust funds to truly take them off budget.

Medicare

There is more urgency today in dealing with the Medicare program because of the projections of financial shortfalls for the Part A trust fund by the turn of the century. The most important reform should be to slow the growth rate of health care spending. This is inextricably linked to the growth rate of overall health care spending in the United States and any solution for Medicare will be most effective if it is explicitly or implicitly part of a systemwide approach. Indeed, Medicare has done a better job of holding down growth in costs than other parts of our health care system since the mid-1980s (Moon and Zuckerman 1995).

Truly reducing health care spending growth means tackling issues such as the diffusion of new technology—a challenging area that will affect all Americans (Huskamp and Newhouse 1994). Substantial improvements could be made in the current Medicare program by adopting some of the innovations now underway in the private sector, including better oversight of certain benefits like home health care services and outpatient hospital services. Such efforts are important even if Medicare eventually shifts toward a private managed-care focus, since the transition would take a long time and some basic fall-back Medicare program is likely to remain indefinitely. In addition, if problems with determining how much to pay private plans on behalf of beneficiaries can be resolved, some modest savings are likely to be achieved from allowing participation in managed-care arrangements. In other words, Medicare must diligently pursue ways to make the program more efficient and address some of the tough choices about managing the use of care. But none of these changes will likely fully resolve Medicare's problems.

Other efforts to make Medicare more targeted are also warranted. For example, the implicit income-related Part A premium—via the dedication of part of the taxation of Social Security benefits to the Part A trust fund—could be expanded by putting the revenues from additional taxation of these Social Security benefits described earlier into Part A. Further, adding an income-related Part B premium for beneficiaries with incomes above a certain level, or taxing some of the Medicare benefits that people receive as income, could achieve further progressivity in the program. This could be added in addition to a modest expansion in the basic Part B premium.

Improvements in the structure of Medicare's cost sharing could also be undertaken in such a way as to raise the average burdens somewhat, while protecting the most vulnerable. For example, a lower Part A deductible and coinsurance structure would benefit the oldest old more, who are least likely to be able to pay. The Part B deductible could be raised to offset this change, and since its burden is more evenly distributed, it would result in a fairer targeting of cost sharing. Such a change is also more consistent with views regarding where cost sharing is most likely to be effective. This type of approach would likely require that Parts A and B be combined so that the Part A trust fund, which is the one in jeopardy, could be protected. Alternatively, home health benefits could be shifted from Part A's jurisdiction to Part B, thus helping to balance changes in Part A versus those in Part B.[5]

One of the most desirable expansions in Medicare would be to add stop-loss protection, to enhance Medicare's insurance protection and to bring it in line with most private insurance. But such an expansion would be expensive, since so much of the costs of Medicare are attributable to a minority of high-cost beneficiaries. Thus, it is beyond the scope of the modest improvements under consideration here.

An alternative would be to further expand the Qualified Medicare Beneficiary (QMB) program to assist the most vulnerable beneficiaries, raising it, for example, to at least 150 percent of the poverty guidelines. By paying deductibles, premiums, and copayments for such beneficiaries, the QMB program effectively acts as a stop-loss program. Moreover, the presence of the QMB program also makes it more feasible to raise beneficiary contributions through increased premiums and cost sharing when the most needy are protected. An essential element of such an expansion would be to move the QMB program out of Medicaid and into Medicare. Although this would be expensive since states now pay part of the costs of QMB, it would likely increase participation, making the program more effective. It should also help to free up some resources in Medicaid, alleviating the cuts anticipated there.

Raising the age of Medicare eligibility makes most sense as an option if only part of the benefit is reduced—perhaps by assessing a higher premium for those aged 65 to 67, for example. Similarly, Medicare could be improved by allowing younger retirees between the ages of 62 and 65 to enroll, even if at little or no subsidy. These younger retirees now have difficulty affording or obtaining coverage if they do not have retiree benefits from a former employer. Particularly given the failure of broader health care reform and the cutbacks in retiree health benefits that seem to be on the way, such an expansion could be helpful to older persons at little additional cost.

Finally, a small payroll tax shift from Social Security to Medicare might be in order, changing the balance between the two funds, but not raising the overall percentages of payroll subject to tax.[6] Such changes have been undertaken a number of times in the past to help realign trust fund balances. The percentage could increase, for example, from 1.45 to 1.6 percent for both employers and employees. This would speed up the trust fund problem for Social Security while providing relief to Medicare, putting the two trust funds on a more equal footing.

Long-term Care

Finally, we favor a gradual, modest expansion of public long-term care services. Of particular importance is a home and community-based long-term care program, with substantial cost-sharing requirements and strong federal controls (either in Medicaid or as a standalone program). Some of the asset requirements for nursing home benefits under Medicaid could also be eased. This expansion could be financed by a combination of contributions from beneficiaries, a small increase in revenues from other sources (such as a dedicated "sin tax"), savings in Medicaid from moving the QMB program to Medicare, and a shifting of some resources from Social Security savings.[7] Since the savings from Social Security that would be dedicated to this program would come largely from high-income individuals, it should be possible to ease the welfare nature of the current system for providing public support for long-term care while recognizing public concerns about funding too many benefits for the well-off elderly.

Linkages

From the preceding discussion, a number of the critical linkages we see across these three programs should be apparent. Medicare premiums are now taken out of Social Security benefits, so that to many beneficiaries, a cut in the Social Security COLA or a rise in Part B premiums will have exactly the same impact on the family budget. The Part A Medicare trust fund now benefits from an infusion of revenues from the taxation of Social Security benefits—a linkage we propose to increase. And more than 1 in 10 Medicare beneficiaries receive Medicaid benefits that supplement their medical care needs.

On balance, we would use some savings from Social Security to help both Medicare and a long-term care benefit (perhaps through the Medicaid program). And we would relieve Medicaid of the QMB burden, putting it in Medicare where it most logically belongs. Our rationale is that it makes sense to view these programs as a whole in terms of their desired impact on the elderly. It is often easier to change Social Security to make it more progressive—along with some modest changes in Medicare. But viewing these programs together also means that if we move on all fronts to expand progressivity, it is possible to avoid tipping the balance too far, thus losing the advantages of universality that help make Medicare and Social Security so popular. This is yet another reason to consider the combined impact of policy changes.

Further, if modest changes in each program can be made to avoid the radical restructuring of any one, that is to the ultimate advantage of older Americans. That is, if Social Security is kept totally out of discussions of balancing the federal budget for the next 10 to 15 years, reductions in Medicare and Medicaid are likely to be even greater than would otherwise be the case—and greater than is desirable.

Finally, the trust funds for the two social insurance programs, Social Security and Medicare, are now out of sync. Social Security is sound for at least 30 years, while Medicare faces a short-term crisis. Changes in Medicare spending that reflect the need to slow health care spending are important and urgently needed. But, it is also reasonable to tap some of the revenues that the two programs share to bring the two trust funds more into balance with each other. The challenge of meeting the needs of the baby boom generation should be undertaken simultaneously in Medicare and Social Security.

The most important linkage to consider, however, is the issue of the well-being of Americans of all ages and an understanding of the effects on that well-being of policy changes in programs crucial to older Americans. Since many of the large changes being contemplated in the current discussion about entitlement reform will alter the economic well-being of seniors directly, we should evaluate what changes are equitable and desirable in the broader context of the well-being of all Americans. We need to move beyond the myths about the elderly and the myths about entitlements in order to allow an honest discussion of options and impacts, one in which numerous possibilities are examined and debated to ensure that reasoned choices are made.

Notes

1. There are, of course, limits even here since, for example, Social Security has not been able to fully eliminate poverty among the elderly.

2. Medicaid's benefits for younger families also ought to be part of that equation.

3. Although our focus here is on the elderly, such changes might also be thought of as means for improving the outlook for the Disability Insurance trust fund as well, for example.

4. Currently, raising this tax limit increases future liabilities substantially. If combined with a change in the formula for calculating benefits, subjecting more of wages to the payroll tax would have a greater long-run impact on the health of the Social Security trust funds.

5. In the short run, a number of adjustments can be made to protect the Part A trust funds to allow adoption of a more orderly set of reforms to Medicare.

6. A balancing of the dedication of revenues from the taxation of Social Security benefits and this payroll tax shift would be needed to determine the appropriate mix.

7. Altogether, the increases in resources to help support long-term care and the QMB shift to Medicare should help states' financial outlook not only in supporting long-term care but also in the important task of helping younger families.

REFERENCES

Aaron, Henry J., and Gary Burtless. 1994. *Retirement and Economic Behavior: Brookings Studies in Social Economics.* Washington, D.C.: Brookings Institution.

Achenbaum, Andrew. 1986. *Social Security: Visions and Revisions.* New York: Cambridge University Press.

Agency for Health Care Policy and Research. 1990. "Use of Home and Community Services by Persons Ages 65 and Older with Functional Difficulties." Research Findings 5. Washington, D.C.: U.S. Department of Health and Human Services, September.

American Association of Retired Persons/Public Policy Institute. 1994. *Coming Up Short: Increasing Out-of-Pocket Health Spending by Older Americans.* Washington, D.C.: Author, April.

Anderson, Martin. 1978. *Welfare.* Stanford, Calif.: Hoover Institution.

Andrews, Emily S. 1988. "An Overview of the Employee Benefit System." Paper presented to the National Research Council Panel on Employer Policies and Working Families, Committee on Women's Employment and Related Social Issues. Washington, D.C.: Employee Benefit Research Institute.

Ball, Robert. 1988. "Social Security across Generations." In *Social Security and Economic Well-being across Generations.* Edited by John Gist. Washington, D.C.: American Association of Retired Persons, Public Policy Institute.

————. 1978. *Social Security Today and Tomorrow.* New York: Columbia University Press.

Bernheim, Douglas. 1993. *Is the Baby Boom Generation Preparing Adequately for Retirement?* Princeton, N.J.: Princeton University.

Bipartisan Commission on Entitlement and Tax Reform. 1995. *Final Report to the President.* Washington, D.C.: U.S. Government Printing Office, January.

Board of Trustees, Federal Hospital Insurance Trust Fund. 1995. *1995 Annual Report of the Hospital Insurance Trust Fund.* Washington, D.C.: U.S. Government Printing Office.

Board of Trustees, Federal Old-Age and Survivors Insurance and Disability Trust Funds. 1995. *1995 Annual Report of the Federal Old-Age and*

Survivors Insurance and Disability Trust Funds. Washington, D.C.: U.S. Government Printing Office.

―――――. 1984. *1984 Annual Report of the Federal Old-Age and Survivors Insurance and Disability Trust Funds.* Washington, D.C.: U.S. Government Printing Office.

Board of Trustees, Federal Supplementary Medical Insurance Fund. 1995. *1995 Annual Report of the Board of Trustees of the Federal Supplementary Medical Insurance Trust Fund.* Washington, D.C.: U.S. Government Printing Office.

Bondar, Joseph. 1989. "Beneficiaries Affected by the Annual Earnings Test, 1989." *Social Security Bulletin* 56(1):20–28.

Boskin, Michael J. 1986. *Too Many Promises: The Uncertain Future of Social Security.* Homewood, Ill.: Twentieth Century Fund.

Bosworth, Barry. 1995. "The Social Security Trust Fund: How Big? How Managed?" Paper Presented to the National Academy of Social Insurance Conference, January, Washington, D.C.

Brown, Randall, Dolores Clement, Jerrold Hill, Sheldon Retchin, and Jeanette Bergeron. 1993. "Do Health Maintenance Organizations Work for Medicare?" *Health Care Financing Review* 15 (Fall):7–23.

Burkhauser, Richard V. 1994. "Protecting the Most Vulnerable: A Proposal to Improve Social Security Insurance for Older Women." *The Gerontologist* 34(2):148–49.

Burkhauser, Richard V., and Karen C. Holden (eds.). 1982. *A Challenge to Social Security: The Changing Roles of Women and Men in American Society.* New York: Academic Press.

Burkhauser, Richard V., and Timothy M. Smeeding. 1994. *Social Security Reform: A Budget Neutral Approach to Reducing Older Women's Disproportionate Risk of Poverty.* Syracuse, N.Y.: Syracuse University, Center for Policy Research, Maxwell School.

Burkhauser, Richard V., Greg J. Duncan, and Richard Hauser. 1994. "Sharing Prosperity across the Age Distribution: A Comparison of the United States and Germany in the 1980s." *The Gerontologist* 34(2):150–60.

Carlson, Elliott. 1994. *News Bulletin.* Washington, D.C.: American Association of Retired Persons.

CBO. *See* U.S. Congressional Budget Office.

Census Bureau. *See* U.S. Bureau of the Census.

Chernick, Howard, and Andrew Reschovsky. 1995. "The Taxation of Social Security." *National Tax Journal* 38(2):141–53.

Christensen, Sandra. 1992. "The Subsidy Provided under Medicare to Current Enrollees." *Journal of Health Politics, Policy and Law* 17(2, Summer):255–64.

Chulis, George S., Franklin J. Eppig, Mary O. Hogan, Daniel R. Waldo, and Ross H. Arnett, III. 1993. "Health Insurance and the Elderly: Data from MCBS." *Health Care Financing Review* 14(Spring):163–81.

Cohen, Lee, 1992. *Old Age Insurance: Who Gets What for Their Money?* Issue

Brief No. 15. Washington, D.C.: American Association of Retired Persons, Public Policy Institute, October.

Cohen, Lee, and Laurel Beedon. 1994. "Options for Balancing the OASDI Trust Funds for the Long-Term." *Journal of Aging and Social Policy* 6(1 & 2); 77–93.

Concord Coalition. 1994. *The Zero Deficit Plan: A Plan for Eliminating the Federal Budget Deficit by the Year 2000*. Washington, D.C.: Author.

Congressional Research Service. 1994. *Entitlements and Other Mandatory Spending*. CRS Report for Congress. Washington, D.C.: Author, April.

————. 1989. *Health Insurance and the Uninsured: Background Data and Analysis*. U.S. Senate Committee on Education and Labor, Committee Print 100-2, pp. 122–23.

Coronel, Susan, and Diane Fulton. 1995. *Long-Term Care Insurance in 1993*. Washington, D.C.: Health Insurance Association of America, March.

Coughlin, Terri, John Holahan, and Leighton Ku. 1994. *Medicaid since 1980*. Washington, D.C.: Urban Institute Press.

Danziger, Sheldon, Jacques van der Gaag, Eugene Smolensky, and Michael Taussig. 1984. "Income Transfers and the Economic Status of the Elderly." In *Economic Transfers in the United States*, edited by Marilyn Moon. Chicago: University of Chicago Press.

Day, Christine L. 1993. "Public Opinion toward Costs and Benefits of Social Security and Medicare." *Research on Aging* 15(3):279–98.

Doty, Pamela, Korbin Liu, and Joshua Wiener. 1985. "An Overview of Long Term Care." *Health Care Financing Review* 5(Spring):69–78.

Drabek, John, and Eugene Moyer. 1994. "The Elderly with Disabilities: At Risk for High Health Care Costs." ASPE Research Notes. Washington, D.C.: U.S. Department of Health and Human Services, February.

Duncan, Greg J. 1984. "Years of Poverty, Years of Plenty." Ann Arbor: University of Michigan, Survey Research Institute, Institute for Social Research.

Etheredge, Lynn. 1995. "Reengineering Medicare: From Bill-Paying Insurer to Accountable Purchaser." Report prepared for Health Insurance Reform Project. Washington, D.C.: George Washington University, June.

Families USA. 1992. "The Medicare Buy-in: Still a Government Secret." Washington, D.C.: Families USA Foundation. Photocopy.

Feder, Judith, Marilyn Moon, and William Scanlon. 1987. "Medicare Reform: Nibbling at Catastrophic Costs." *Health Affairs* 6(Winter):5–19.

Feldstein, Martin S. 1987. "Should Social Security Benefits Be Means-Tested?" *Journal of Political Economy* 95(3):468–84.

————. 1974. "Social Security, Induced Retirement, and Aggregate Capital Accumulation." *Journal of Political Economy* 83 (September/October): 905–96.

Ferber, Marianne A. 1993. "Women's Employment and the Social Security System." *Social Security Bulletin* 56(3):33–55.

Fields, Gary S., and Olivia S. Mitchell. 1984. "The Effects of Social Security

Reforms on Retirement Ages and Retirement Income." *Journal of Public Economics* (25):143–59.

Freudenheim, Milt. 1995. "Medicare, Jot This Down." *New York Times*, May 31: D1, D4.

GAO. *See* U.S. General Accounting Office.

Gist, John R. 1992. "Did Tax Reform Hurt the Elderly?" *The Gerontologist* 32(4):472–77.

———. 1990a. "Federal and State Income Tax Reform and Older Americans." *Policy Studies Journal* 19(1):40–58.

———. 1990b. "Tax Reform, Revenue Windfalls, and Elderly Taxpayers." *Environment and Planning* (8):41–52.

———. 1989. *The Taxation of Social Security: Issues and Policy Options* (pp. 1–18). Issue Paper. Washington, D.C.: American Association of Retired Persons, Public Policy Institute, July.

Gist, John, and Janemarie Mulvey. 1990. "Marginal Tax Rates and Older Taxpayers." *Tax Notes* 49(6):679–94.

Grad, Susan. 1994. *Income of the Population 55 or Older, 1992*. Social Security Administration, Office of Policy, Washington, D.C.: U.S. Government Printing Office.

Guralnick, Jack. 1991. "Prospects for the Compression of Morbidity: The Challenge Posed by Increasing Disability in the Years prior to Death." *Journal of Aging and Health* 3(May):138–54.

Hage, David, and Robert F. Black. 1995. "New Surgery for Health Care." *U.S. News & World Report*, February 27:68–69.

Hewitt Associates. 1994. "Salaried Employee Benefits Provided by Major U.S. Employers." Lincolnshire, IL. Author.

Holahan, John, Teresa Coughlin, Korbin Liu, Leighton Ku, Crystal Kuntz, Martcia Wade, and Susan Wall. Forthcoming. "Cutting Medicaid Spending in Response to Budget Caps." Report prepared for Kaiser Commission on the Future of Medicaid. Photocopy.

Hurd, Michael D. 1989. "The Economic Status of the Elderly." *Science* 224(1):659–64.

Huskamp, Haiden A., and Joseph P. Newhouse. 1994. "Is Health Spending Slowing Down?" *Health Affairs* 13(Winter):32–38.

Ippolito, Richard A. 1990. "Toward Explaining Earlier Retirement after 1970." *Industrial and Labor Relations Review* 43(5):556–69.

Juster, Thomas, and Marilyn Moon. Forthcoming. "Economic Status Variables and the HRS." In *Journal of Human Resources.*

Kahn, Katherine, Lisa V. Rubenstein, David Draper, Jacqueline Kosecoff, William H. Rogers, Emmett B. Keeler, and Robert H. Brook. 1990. "The Effects of the DRG-Based Prospective Payment System on Quality of Care for Hospitalized Medicare Patients." *Journal of the American Medical Association* 264(15):1953–55.

Keenan, Marianne. 1988. *Changing Needs for Long Term Care: A Chartbook.* Washington, D.C.: American Association of Retired Persons, Public Policy Institute.

Kenney, Genevieve. 1991. "Understanding the Effects of the PPS on Medicare Home Health Use." *Inquiry* 28(2):129–39.

————. 1990. "Understanding the Reasons for Growth in Medicare Home Health Use between 1983 and 1985." Report prepared under Robert Wood Johnson Foundation Grant no. 12548. Photocopy, August.

Kenney, Genevieve, and Marilyn Moon. 1995. "Medicare Subacute Care Services and Enrollee Characteristics." Report prepared under Health Care Financing Administration Contract no. 500-89-0064. Photocopy.

Kollman, Geoffrey. 1992. *Social Security: The Relationship of Taxes and Benefits*. Congressional Research Service Report to Congress. Washington, D.C.: Congressional Research Service, December 16.

Korcyzyk, Sophie M. 1993. "Gender Issues in Employer Pension Policy." *Pensions in a Changing Economy*. Washington, D.C.: Employee Benefits Research Institute and National Academy on Aging.

Langwell, Kathryn, and James Hadley. 1989. "Evaluation of the Medicare Competition Demonstrations." *Health Care Financing Review* 11(Winter):65–79.

Lefkowitz, Diane, and Alan Monheit. 1991. *Health Insurance, Use of Health Services, and Health Care Expenditures*. AHCPR Pub. No. 92-0017, National Medical Expenditure Survey Research Findings 12. Rockville, MD.: U.S. Public Health Service, Agency for Health Care Policy and Research.

Leimer, Dean R., and Selig D. Lesnoy. 1982. "Social Security and Private Saving: New Time-Series Evidence." *Journal of Political Economy* 90(3):606–29.

Liska, David, Karen Obermaier, Barbara Lyons, and Peter Long. 1995. *Medicaid Expenditures and Beneficiaries: State Profiles and Trends, 1984–1993*. Report prepared for Kaiser Commission on the Future of Medicaid, July.

Mahoney, Kevin. 1990. "The Connecticut Partnership for Long-Term Care." *Generations* 14(Spring 1990):71–72.

Manton, Kenneth, Larry Corder, and Eric Stallard. 1993. "Estimates of Change in Chronic Disability and Institutional Incidence and Prevalence Rates in the U.S. Elderly Population from the 1982, 1984, and 1989 National Long Term Care Survey." *Journals of Gerontology: Social Sciences* 48(4):S153–66.

Moon, Marilyn. Forthcoming. "Treatment of Long-Term Care in the 1994 Health Care Reform Proposals." Report prepared for Kaiser Commission on the Future of Medicaid. Photocopy.

————. 1995. "Health Care Spending and the Federal Budget." Testimony before the Committee on the Budget, U.S. Senate 104th Cong. 1st Sess. February.

————. 1993. *Medicare Now and in the Future*. Washington, D.C.: Urban Institute Press.

————. 1987. "The Elderly's Access to Health Care Services: The Crude and

Subtle Impacts of Medicare Changes." *Social Justice Research* 1(3):361–75.

Moon, Marilyn, and Stephen Zuckerman. 1995. "Are Private Insurers Really Controlling Spending Better than Medicare?" Henry J. Kaiser Family Foundation Discussion Paper, July. Photocopy.

National Academy of Social Insurance. 1988. *The Social Security Benefit Notch: A Study.* Report prepared for the Committee on Finance, Subcommittee on Social Security and Family Policy, Washington, November.

National Research Council, Panel on Poverty and Family Assistance. 1995. *Measuring Poverty: A New Approach*, edited by Constance Citro and Robert Michael. Washington, D.C.: National Academy Press.

Neumann, Peter, Mimi Bernardin, Ellen Bayer, and William Evans. 1994. *Identifying Barriers to Elderly Participation in the Qualified Medicare Beneficiary Program.* Bethesda, MD: Project HOPE Center for Health Affairs, August.

O'Sullivan, Jennifer. 1995. "Medicare: Financing the Part A Hospital Insurance Program." Congressional Research Service report to Congress. Washington, D.C.: Congressional Research Service, May. Photocopy.

Paine, Thomas. 1994. "Appraising Public Policy for Private Retirement Plans." *Pension Funding and Taxation: Implications for Tomorrow.* Washington, D.C.: Employee Benefits Research Institute.

Pattison, David, and David E. Harrington. 1993. "Proposals to Modify the Taxation of Social Security Benefits: Options and Distributional Effects." *Social Security Bulletin* 56(2):3–21.

Pauly, Mark. 1990. "The Rational Nonpurchase of Long-Term-Care Insurance." *Journal of Political Economy* 98:153–68.

Pepper Commission (U.S. Bipartisan Commission on Comprehensive Health Care). 1990. *A Call for Action.* Washington, D.C.: U.S. Government Printing Office.

Peterson, Peter G. 1993. *Facing Up: How to Rescue the Economy from Crushing Debt and Restore the American Dream.* New York: Simon & Schuster.

Peterson, Peter, and Neil Howe. 1988. *On Borrowed Time.* New York: Simon & Schuster.

Physician Payment Review Commission. 1994. *Annual Report to Congress.* Washington, D.C.: U.S. Government Printing Office.

Prospective Payment Assessment Commission. 1994. *Report and Recommendations to the Congress.* Washington, D.C.: U.S. Government Printing Office, March.

Radner, Daniel. 1993. "An Assessment of the Economic Status of the Aged." *Studies in Income Distribution* 16(May), entire issue.

———. 1987. "Money Incomes of Aged and Nonaged Family Units, 1967–1984." *Social Security Bulletin* 50(August):9–28.

Ratner, Jonathan. 1995. *Medicare: Rapid Spending Growth Calls for More Prudent Purchasing.* Washington, D.C.: General Accounting Office.

Reno, Virginia P. 1993. "The Role of Pensions in Retirement Income." *Pensions* in a Changing Economy. Washington, D.C.: Employee Benefits Research Institute and National Academy on Aging.

Rice, Thomas, Kathleen Thomas, and William Weissert. 1991. "The Effect of Owning Private Long-Term Care Insurance Policies on Out-of-Pocket Costs." Health Services Research 25(February): 907–34.

Rich, Spencer. 1995. "Plan Deepens Cuts for Future Retirees." Washington Post May 22, 1995, p. A21.

Rivlin, Alice, and Joshua Wiener. 1988. Caring for the Disabled Elderly. Washington, D.C.: Brookings Institution.

Ross, Christine, Sheldon Danziger, and Eugene Smolensky. 1987. "Interpreting Changes in the Economic Status of the Elderly, 1949–1979." Contemporary Policy Issues 5:98–112.

Ross, Jane L., and Melinda M. Upp. 1993. "Treatment of Women in the U.S. Social Security System." Social Security Bulletin 56(3):56–67.

Ruggles, Patricia. 1990. Drawing the Line: Alternative Poverty Measures and Their Implications for Public Policy. Washington, D.C.: Urban Institute Press.

Sablehaus, John, and Joyce Manchester. 1994. "Baby Boomers and Their Parents: How Does Their Economic Well-Being Compare in Middle Age?" Paper presented at the 1994 American Economic Association meetings, Boston.

Sammartino, Frank J., and Richard A. Kasten. 1985. "The Distributional Consequences of Taxing Social Security Benefits: Current Law and Alternative Schemes." Journal of Post-Keynsian Economics. 8(1): entire issue.

Sammartino, Frank J., and Roberton Williams. 1991. "Trends in Income and Federal Taxes of the Elderly." Paper presented at the 13th Annual Research Conference of the Association for Public Policy Analysis and Management, October 24–26. Washington, D.C.

Schulz, James, Guy Carrin, Hans Krupp, Manfred Peschke, Elliott Sclar, and J. Van Steenberge. 1974. Providing Adequate Retirement Income: Pension Reform in the United States and Abroad. Hanover, N.H.: University Press of New England.

Seib, Gerald. 1995. "How the GOP Seeks to Elude the Medicare Wreck." Wall Street Journal, May 3: A16.

Silverman, Celia, and Paul Yakoboski. 1994. "Public and Private Pensions Today: An Overview of the System." Pension Funding and Taxation. Washington, D.C.: Employee Benefits Research Institute.

Simpson, Alan. 1995. "The Kerrey Simpson Proposal." 104th Congress, 1st sess. Photocopy.

Smeeding, Timothy M. 1994. "Improving Supplemental Security Income." In Social Welfare Policy at the Crossroads: Rethinking the Roles of Social Insurance, Tax Expenditures, Mandates, and Means-Testing, edited by Robert Friedland, Lynn Etheredge, and Bruce Vladeck, pp. 97–108. Washington, D.C.: National Academy of Social Insurance.

————. 1986. "Nonmoney Income and the Elderly: The Case of the 'Tweeners.' " *Journal of Policy Analysis and Management* 5(Summer):707–24.

————. 1984. "Approaches to Measuring and Valuing In-Kind Subsidies and the Distribution of their Benefits." In *Economic Transfers in the United States*, edited by Marilyn Moon. National Bureau of Economic Research Income and Wealth Conference. Chicago: University of Chicago Press.

————. 1982. *Alternative Methods for Valuing Selected Link and Transfers and Measuring Their Impact on Poverty*. U.S. Bureau of the Census Technical Paper #50. Washington, D.C.: U.S. Government Printing Office.

Smith, David G. 1992. *Paying for Medicare: The Politics of Reform*. Hawthorne, N.Y.: Aldine de Gruyter.

Starobin, Paul. 1994. "Sorting Out All the Talk of a Tax Cut." *National Journal*, September 17:2149–50.

Steuerle, C. Eugene. 1992. *The Tax Decade: How Taxes Came to Dominate the Public Agenda*. Washington, D.C.: Urban Institute Press.

Steuerle, C. Eugene, and Jon M. Bakija. 1994. *Retooling Social Security for the 21st Century: Right and Wrong Approaches to Reform* (p. 11–31). Washington, D.C.: Urban Institute Press.

Sullivan, Cynthia, Marianne Miller, Roger Feldman, and Bryan Dowd. 1992. "Employer-Sponsored Health Insurance in 1991." *Health Affairs* 11(Winter):172–85.

Swoboda, Frank. 1995. "The Unforseen Peril in Retirement Planning." *Washington Post*, May 14: H9.

Taueber, Cynthia. 1992. *Sixty-Five Plus in America*. Current Population Reports, Special Studies, P23–178. Washington, D.C.: U.S. Department of Commerce, Bureau of the Census.

U.S. Bureau of the Census. 1995. *Income, Poverty, and Valuation of Noncash Benefits: 1993*. Current Population Reports, ser. P60, no. 188. Washington, D.C. U.S. Government Printing Office.

————. 1993a. *Money Income of Households, Families, and Persons in the United States: 1992*. Current Population Reports, ser. P-60, no. 174. Washington, D.C.: U.S. Government Printing Office.

————. 1993b. *Poverty in the United States: 1992*. Current Population Reports, ser. P-60, no. 185. Washington, D.C.: U.S. Government Printing Office.

————. 1993c. *Statistical Abstract of the U.S.: 1993*. Washington, D.C.: U.S. Government Printing Office.

————. 1991. *Poverty in the United States: 1988 and 1989*. Current Population Reports, ser. P-60, no. 171. Washington, D.C.: U.S. Government Printing Office.

————. 1984. *Characteristics of the Population Below the Poverty Level: 1982*. Current Population Reports, ser. P-60, no. 144. Washington, D.C.: U.S. Government Printing Office.

U.S. Congressional Budget Office. 1995a. "Baseline: Medicare." Staff memorandum. Washington, D.C.: Author, March.

————. 1995b. *Reducing the Deficit: Spending and Revenue Options.* Washington, D.C.: U.S. Government Printing Office, February.

————. 1995c. "Baseline: Medicare." Staff memorandum. Washington, D.C.: Author, January.

————. 1994a. *Is the Growth in the CPI a Biased Measure in the Cost of Living?* Washington, D.C.: Author, October.

————. 1994b. *Implications of Revising Social Security's Investment Policies.* Washington, D.C.: Author, September.

————. 1994c. *The Economic and Budget Outlook: Fiscal Years 1995–1999.* Washington, D.C.: U.S. Government Printing Office, January.

————. 1994d. *Reducing Entitlement Spending.* Washington, D.C.: U.S. Government Printing Office.

————. 1993. *Baby Boomers in Retirement: An Early Perspective.* Washington, D.C.: Author, September.

————. 1992. "Mandatory Spending: Trends and Sources of Growth." Staff memorandum. Washington, D.C.: Author, July.

————. 1991. *Universal Health Insurance Coverage Using Medicare's Payment Rates.* Washington, D.C.: U.S. Government Printing Office, December.

————. 1989. *The Economic Status of the Elderly.* Washington, D.C.: Author, May.

U.S. Department of Commerce. 1993. *Population Projections of the United States by Age, Sex, Race, and Hispanic Origin: 1993 to 2050.* Pub. no. P25-1104. Washington, D.C.: Author, November.

U.S. Department of Health and Human Services. 1994. *Cost Estimates for the Long Term Care Provisions under the Health Security Act.* Washington, D.C.: Author, March.

————. 1993. "Advance Report on Final Mortality Statistics, 1990." *Monthly Vital Statistics Report.* Washington, D.C.: Author.

U.S. General Accounting Office. 1993. *Medicaid Estate Planning.* Pub. no. HRD-93-29R. Washington, D.C.: Author, July.

————. 1991. *Medigap Insurance: Better Consumer Protection Should Result from 1990 Changes to Baucus Amendment.* Pub. no. HRD-91-49. Washington, D.C.: Author.

————. 1981. *A Glossary of Terms Used in the Federal Budget Process and Related Accounting, Economic, and Tax Terms.* Washington, D.C.: Author, March.

U.S. House Committee on Ways and Means. 1995. "Taxation of Social Security Benefits." 104th Congress, 1st sess. Photocopy.

————. 1994. *1994 Green Book: Overview of Entitlement Programs.* U.S. House of Representatives. Washington, D.C.: U.S. Government Printing Office.

————. 1993. *1993 Green Book: Overview of Entitlement Programs.* U.S.

House of Representatives. Washington, D.C.: U.S. Government Printing Office.

————. 1992. *1992 Green Book: Background Material and Data on Programs within the Jurisdiction of the Committee on Ways and Means.* U.S. House of Representatives. Washington, D.C.: U.S. Government Printing Office, June.

U.S. Social Security Admininstration. 1988. *Social Security Bulletin.* Washington, D.C.: Author, December.

Weaver, Carolyn L., ed. 1990. *Social Security's Looming Surpluses: Prospects and Implications.* American Enterprise Institute Study no. 511. Washington, D.C.: American Enterprise Institute Press.

Weinberg, Daniel, and Enrique Lamas. 1993. "Some Experimental Results on Alternate Poverty Measures." Paper presented at the 1993 Winter Meetings of the American Statistical Association, Alexandria, VA, December.

Wiener, Joshua M., Laurel Illston, and Raymond Hanley. 1994. *Sharing the Burden: Strategies for Public and Private Long-Term Care Insurance.* Washington, D.C.: Brookings Institution.

Wiatrowski, William J. 1993. "Factors Affecting Retirement Income." *Monthly Labor Review* 116(3):25–35.

Wines, Michael. 1995. "Gingrich Promises Big but Painless Cuts in Medicare." *New York Times,* May 8: A1, A15.

Wolff, Edward. 1987. "Estimate of Household Wealth Inequality in the U.S., 1962–1983." *Review of Income and Wealth* 33(September):231–56.

Yeas, Martynas, and Susan Grad. 1987. "Income of Retirement Aged Persons in the United States." *Social Security Bulletin* 50:5–14.

Zedlewski, Sheila. 1988. "The Increasing Fiscal Burden on the Elderly." In *Social Security and Economic Well-being across Generations,* edited by John Gist. Washington, D.C.: American Association of Retired Persons, Public Policy Institute.

Zedlewski, Sheila, Robert Barnes, Martha Burt, Timothy McBride, and Jack Meyer. 1990. *The Needs of the Elderly in the 21st Century.* Urban Institute Report 90-5. Washington, D.C.: Urban Institute Press.

Zuckerman, Stephen, and Diana Verrilli. 1995. "The Medicare Relative Value Scale and Private Payers: The Potential Impact on Physician Payments." Report prepared under Health Care Financing Administration Contract no. 500-92-0024, D.O. #4. Photocopy.

INDEX

Marilyn Moon is a Senior Fellow with the Health Policy Center of the Urban Institute. Prior to this position, she served as Director of the Public Policy Institute of the American Association of Retired Persons and as a senior analyst at the Congressional Budget Office. She has written extensively on health policy, policy for the elderly, and income distribution. Her current work focuses on health system reform and financing. Since October 1993, she has been writing a periodic column for the Health section of the *Washington Post* on health reform and health coverage issues.

Janemarie Mulvey is a Senior Associate at the Center for Health Policy Studies in Maryland. She was previously a research associate at the Urban Institute, where she worked on issues on simulating health policy proposals at the state level, and measures of poverty and out-of-pocket health care spending by the elderly. She has previously worked for the American Association of Retired Persons and for Data Resources Inc.